I0815283

To:

From:

Date:

Visit Christian Art Gifts, Inc., at www.christianartgifts.com.

My First Devotional: Meaningful Time with God for Little Ones

Published by Christian Art Gifts, Inc., Bloomingdale, IL, USA.

First edition 2024.

Designed by Allison Sowers.

Cover and interior images used under license from Shutterstock.com.

ISBN 978-1-63952-670-3

Printed in Vietnam.

29 28 27 26 25 24
10 9 8 7 6 5 4 3 2 1

Printed in Binh Phuoc, Vietnam
MARCH 2024
Print Run: PUR404097

Christie Thomas

Preface

Can our little ones really know Jesus? Oh sure, we know they can parrot Bible-story facts back at us, but do they know that the Bible is relevant for their everyday lives? What do Adam and Eve have to do with your two-year-old's tantrum or Jesus' conversation with Mary and Martha when your child's hamster dies? Everything.

Second Timothy 3:14-15 is a good summary of my vision for teaching little ones the Bible:

"But as for you, continue in what you have learned and have become convinced of, because you know those from whom you learned it, and how from infancy you have known the Holy Scriptures, which are able to make you wise for salvation through faith in Christ Jesus (NIV)."

Timothy's faith was learned from his grandmother, Lois, and his mother, Eunice. From his earliest days, Timothy was steeped in the knowledge of God, and because of this, he was one of Jesus' earliest followers. Not only that, but he became a leader in the church at a very young age.

The Bible is clear that our little ones can know the Scripture from early childhood, and that it will make them wise for salvation through faith in Christ Jesus. Isn't that beautiful?

But the question is, how do we teach our 2- to 6-year-olds the content of this amazing but rather overwhelming book? Usually, we resort to children's picture Bibles, right? I love a good children's picture Bible and have many on my shelf at home, but if all we ever read are picture Bibles, we are missing a whole lot of amazing Scripture that is completely relevant to our toddlers and preschoolers. When we paraphrase Scripture and blast through a new story every day, we miss out on so many amazing details that can spark their faith and imaginations.

So how do you do it?

You're holding the answer in your hands: This book is essentially a simple, interactive, fun Bible study for little kids.

Here's what you'll find inside this book:

1) A single Bible passage per week

Focusing on a single passage each week has many benefits:

- If your child is squirmy one day, you know you have four other days to help them connect!
- You can go deeper into each passage without it feeling over-whelming to you or your child.
- It takes less time each day but adds up to more total time learning that single passage.
- If you want to, you can pair your weekly Sunday school lesson with this book.

2) A variety of learning styles

In general, young children learn through participatory movement and imaginative interaction. To that end, I have incorporated a large array of learning styles into my devotionals. Children will experience God's Word through art, dance, music, Bible memory, Bible reading, object lessons, and more.

For example, instead of just reading about Joshua and the battle of Jericho, you're going to pull out your imaginary trumpet and march around the room seven times. (That's what my kids did with their grandparents, and guess who won't ever forget that lesson?)
This may sound like a lot of work, but keep reading, because the next point is key.

3) Simple lessons

About 75% of the devotions require no supplies, and those that do only involve accessible items like crayons and paper or stuffed animals. When we used this book as a family, we read it in our child's bedroom because they had oodles of stuffed animals, which are hugely useful when acting out Bible stories. If you put a little box of crayons and a blank journal on your child's dresser, you'll have everything you need for about 99 percent of the devotions in this book.

None of the devotions require preparation by the parent. They can be done at bedtime, after supper, in a small group setting, or one-on-one with the child.

4) A focus on reading from the actual Bible

I know this is daunting, but hear me out! I wanted preschoolers to learn straight from the Bible, so they would hear the actual Scripture instead of just my paraphrase. While there is a child-friendly paraphrase included in each lesson, most weeks also include having a parent read a short Bible passage. Usually while this is happening, I have included a small art activity to help children focus. I recommend buying a blank journal that your child can draw in each week. When the journal is full, you will have a beautiful keepsake of your child's spiritual adventure!

The small habits add up

My own boys grew up on this book. In fact, when my eldest went to kindergarten at a Christian school, his teacher was surprised at how much more of the Bible he knew and understood than the many other Christian kids she'd taught over the years.

The reason? It wasn't his supreme intelligence (although I, like most other parents, think my son is quite smart)! Rather, it was our small habit of engaging our sons in God's Word just a few minutes a day, five days per week.

It wasn't always easy. They did their fair share of squirming and giving silly answers to serious questions. But we also made incredible memories, week after week. Our bunk beds became boats and caves, our closet became the tomb where Jesus was buried, and our children experienced the heart-pounding joy of jumping out at their parents and yelling "Jesus is alive!" while we pretended to pass out in shock.

The best part is that as they grew, God was embedding His love and words deep into their hearts and minds, allowing each of them to become "wise for salvation through faith in Christ Jesus."

This is what I want for the children in my church and for young children all over the world. I want them to be wise for salvation because from infancy they have known the Holy Scriptures. I pray that this little book will help your children to become wise for salvation at an early age and become strong Christian leaders as a result.

And while that is happening, I hope you have an absolute blast experiencing the joy and wonder of the Bible through little eyes!

-Christie Thomas

Old Testament

New Testament

Introduction to the Old Testament

The first part of the Bible is called the Old Testament. It's the part of the Bible that was written before Jesus was born.

The Old Testament tells us all about the amazing God who made the world. It also teaches us where all the bad stuff in the world came from (hint: it's not from God) and God's plan for dealing with all the bad stuff. The Old Testament shows us how God picked a special family to use for His great plan and how that family grew and became the Jewish people.

One day, God would come into the world as a little Jewish baby and save us, but that's what the second part of the Bible is all about! For now, let's explore God's amazing plan and the people He showed His love to along the way.

God Makes Light and Dark

Then God said, "Let there be light," and there was light. GENESIS 1:3

In the very beginning, everything was dark all the time. There was no sun or moon, no lightbulbs, not even any flashlights. It was just dark. God decided he wanted to create something, so he did. He didn't need any craft supplies or instructions, he only needed his words. So God said, "Let there be light!"—and suddenly there was light! God decided to call it "daytime" when the light was out and "nighttime" when it was dark. And then he said, "It is good!" This was the very first day.

ACT out the story with your child in a windowless room. Use the light switch to show the difference between day and night.

Have your child close her eyes. Together, imagine what it would be like if it was dark all the time. While your child's eyes are closed, read Genesis 1: 1-5 straight from the Bible. Have your child open her eyes when it says "And there was light!"

SAY: I wonder why God made the light first. If you got to help God create the whole world, what's the first thing you would create?

ASK: Why do you think God created both day AND night? Why not just daytime? Talk about the kinds of things you do during the day and the kinds of things you do during the night.

SAY: Did you know that we can't see colors in the dark? Colors are made from light, so the only time we can see them is when there is light shining! What colors are your favorites?

Prayer

Thank you, God, for creating day and night! I'm so glad that you gave us light and color, as well as darkness for resting. Amen.

God Makes Sky and Water

Then God said, "Let there be something to divide the water in two." **GENESIS 1:6**

The Bible tells us that in the very beginning, instead of a world, there was just water. On the second day, God decided He wanted to change that, so He made a sky to go in between the water. He put some water above the sky, in the clouds. That water would fall out of the sky as fat raindrops, sparkly white snowflakes, and chunks of ice. Down below, the whole world was covered with oceans. And then He said, "It is good!"

Allow your child to play with some water in a sink as you read the story (either the paraphrase or from Genesis 1:6-8).

ASK: What kind of things do we do with water? (swim, drink, get clean) What is your favorite thing to do with water? Let's thank God for all the wonderful things we can do with water!

ASK: Where do we see water in the sky? (rain, snow) Why do we have rain? What does it do for the world? (waters the plants) Thank you, God, for rain!

SAY: Let's pretend we're in one of the oceans God made. Let's put on our scuba gear and go swimming! (pretend to swim around and explore the ocean) **ASK:** What do you see? (point out the various living things you might see in the ocean)

ASK: When our water comes out of the tap, what color is it? Is it clean or dirty? Did you know there are lots of kids in the world who have no clean water to drink? They might have to drink out of mud puddles or places where animals have pooped or even water that has garbage in it. Do you think that kind of water is healthy for children? No way! Let's pray for these children to get some clean water to drink.

Prayer

Thank You, God, for the gift of water. Thank You for all the important things that water does for us. Help us not to take it for granted or to waste what You've given us, but to always be thankful. Amen.

God Makes Land, Plants, and Sea

Then God said, "Let the water under the sky be gathered together so the dry land will appear." And it happened. **GENESIS 1:9**

On the third day, God separated the water by adding some land in between the different oceans. In the middle of the land were seas, lakes, and rivers. On the land and in the water, God put all kinds of plants. From the slimiest seaweed in the bottom of the ocean to the tallest tree on the highest mountain, God made it all! And then He said, "It is good!"

Together with your child, pretend to be a plant. Start crouched down like a tiny seed then slowly grow up into a big plant. **ASK:** What kind of plant are you? I'm a ____________! Did God make you? He sure did!

ASK: Did you know that plants make air for us to breath? I guess they're pretty important! What else do we do with plants? (flowers for decoration, fruits/veggies to eat, big trees for shade...) Thank You God for plants!

SAY: When God made land, He made all kinds of land. There are mountains, valleys, flat grassy lands, deserts, hills, forests, and even lands full of snow and ice! What kind of land would you like to visit?

ASK: How many kinds of plants did God make? Lots and lots! Let's see if we can think of some (tomato plants, apple trees, flowers, grass, Christmas trees, seaweed, moss... [insert your favorite plant here]). Act out some of the plants if you want.) Why do you think God made so many different kinds?

ASK: Do you know what kinds of things plants need to grow? (light, water, dirt) Who made all those things? God did! He made the light on the first day, the water on the second day, and the dirt on the third day. Wow, God sure thought of everything! Isn't He smart?

Prayer

Thank You, God, for making all the biggest things in our world—the mountains, the giant ocean, and the tallest tree. Thank You for making the smallest things too—the tiniest plant in the ocean and the smallest piece of dirt. Amen.

God Makes Sun, Moon, and Stars

Then God said, "Let there be lights in the sky to separate day from night. These lights will be used for signs, seasons, days, and years." **GENESIS 1:14**

Even though God had made day and night, He hadn't put anything in the sky to make light. So on the fourth day, God made the bright yellow sun to give light during the day and the glowing moon and stars to give light at night. And then He said, "It is good!"

Read the paraphrase or Genesis 1:14-19 to your child, then sing "Twinkle, Twinkle" together.

Cup your hands into a pretend telescope and look up at the sky. **ASK:** Do you know how many stars are in the sky? I don't! Let's guess though. Maybe three hundred million billion and ten! Why do you think God made SO many stars? How far away do you think they are?

ASK: Where does the sun go at night? Where does the moon go during the day? Why do you think God wanted us to have a sun and a moon?

SAY: Let's learn something about God's amazing creation—the moon! One of you should stand still and pretend to be the earth, while the other walks in a slow circle around the "earth." **SAY:** Our moon goes all the way around the earth, once a day, every day. (For older kids, you can also explain that the earth travels around the sun.)

Read Psalm 113:3 with your child. **SAY:** This verse tells us that we should praise God all day. Let's praise God right now! Either pray your praises or sing a favorite praise song together.

Prayer

Thank You, God, for putting the sun, moon, and stars in the sky so we can see. You are so great and powerful, how amazing You are! Amen.

God Makes Fish and Birds

Then God said, "Let the water be filled with living things, and let birds fly in the air above the earth." **GENESIS 1:20**

After God made the oceans and the land and the sky, He decided to fill the world up with animals! On day five, He made birds to swoop and glide in the sky and fish to swish around in the water. From enormous whales and toothy sharks to hummingbirds and magpies, God made them all. And then He said, "It is good!"

Read Genesis 1:20-23 or the paraphrase above and act out every kind of creature that you read about. (You'll be alternating underwater creatures and birds several times.)

If you have internet access, go to enature.com/birding/audio.asp and listen to some bird calls. If you have no Internet access, make your own birds calls! Have you heard any of these in your neighborhood? Thank God for the birds in your neighborhood.

Together, imagine you are putting on scuba gear and splashing into the ocean. Swim around and discuss the animals you might find in the ocean. **ASK:** What kinds of animals can you think of that live in the water? I wonder why God made so many kinds. Why do you think God made sharks?

ASK: Have you ever seen a flamingo? How about a penguin? I wonder if God made some birds just to make Him laugh. What fish or birds do you think are silly looking?

Practice saying Genesis 1:31 together. ("God looked at everything He had made, and it was very good.") Try saying it while making a bubbling sound with your finger on your lips (as a fish) and while flapping your arms (as a bird).

Prayer

Thank You, God, for making so many interesting animals to live in the air and water. You are the wonderful God who creates everything for Your joy and our joy. Help us see how amazing Your creation is this week. Amen.

God Makes Land Animals

Then God said, "Let the earth be filled with animals, each producing more of its own kind." **GENESIS 1:24**

On day six, God decided to make some more animals; this time He wanted animals on land. God made every kind of animal you could ever dream of—mischievous monkeys, jaunty giraffes, busy bugs, slow sloths, and terrific turtles. And then He said, "It is good!"

Read Genesis 1:24-25 or the paraphrase above and act out every kind of creature that you read about.

SAY: The Bible says that Adam, the first man, got to name all the animals. Let's collect some stuffed animals and give them all names! What kind of sounds do these animals make?

ASK: If you could ride on any animal in the whole world, which animal would you choose? If you could have any animal as a pet, which animal would you choose? Which animal might be a good pet for God?

Play animal charades with your child: One person pretends to be an animal and the other has to guess what it is! (some ideas: crocodiles, butterflies, snakes, lions, monkeys, mosquitoes) **SAY:** Thanks God for making all these animals!

SAY: The Bible (Genesis 1:28) says people are supposed to rule over animals. That means that we are in charge of them, but we also need to take care of them. Can you think of a way that our family takes care of animals? (Maybe you have a pet, help worms get back into the ground after it rains, put out a bird feeder, or wait for ducks to cross the road.)

Prayer

God, You are so creative, and we thank You for making such an amazing amount of animals for us to enjoy. Help us to look after the animals of the world just like Adam and Eve did. Amen.

God Makes People

Then God said, "Let us make human beings in our image and likeness." **GENESIS 1:26**

God had made all kinds of creatures in all sizes and shapes. But He still wanted to make someone in His image—someone He could talk to. God reached down into the dust and created Adam out of it. When He was done with Adam, He created Eve out of Adam's rib. He gave them hearts for loving, souls for worshiping, minds for thinking, and bodies for playing. When He was done making people, God said, "It is VERY good!" They were His very favorite creation, and He loved them very much.

Have your child draw a picture of a person while you read Genesis 1:26-27 or the paraphrase above. **ASK:** What do you think it means that God made us in the image of God? Why do you think God likes people the best of all His creations?

Use your bodies to have some fun with your child—do the hokey pokey or sing "Head and Shoulders" together! **SAY:** Thanks God for making my whole body!

Draw an outline of a person (or a stick figure). Together with your child, fill in features that belong to them, like the color of eyes and hair or what they're wearing. **SAY:** Thank You, God, for making us different from each other!

Look in a mirror. **ASK:** Did you know that you are God's most special creation? Which part of your body is your favorite?

ASK: How many fingers do you have? How many toes? How many eyes, ears, and noses? How many belly buttons? God made your body so special!

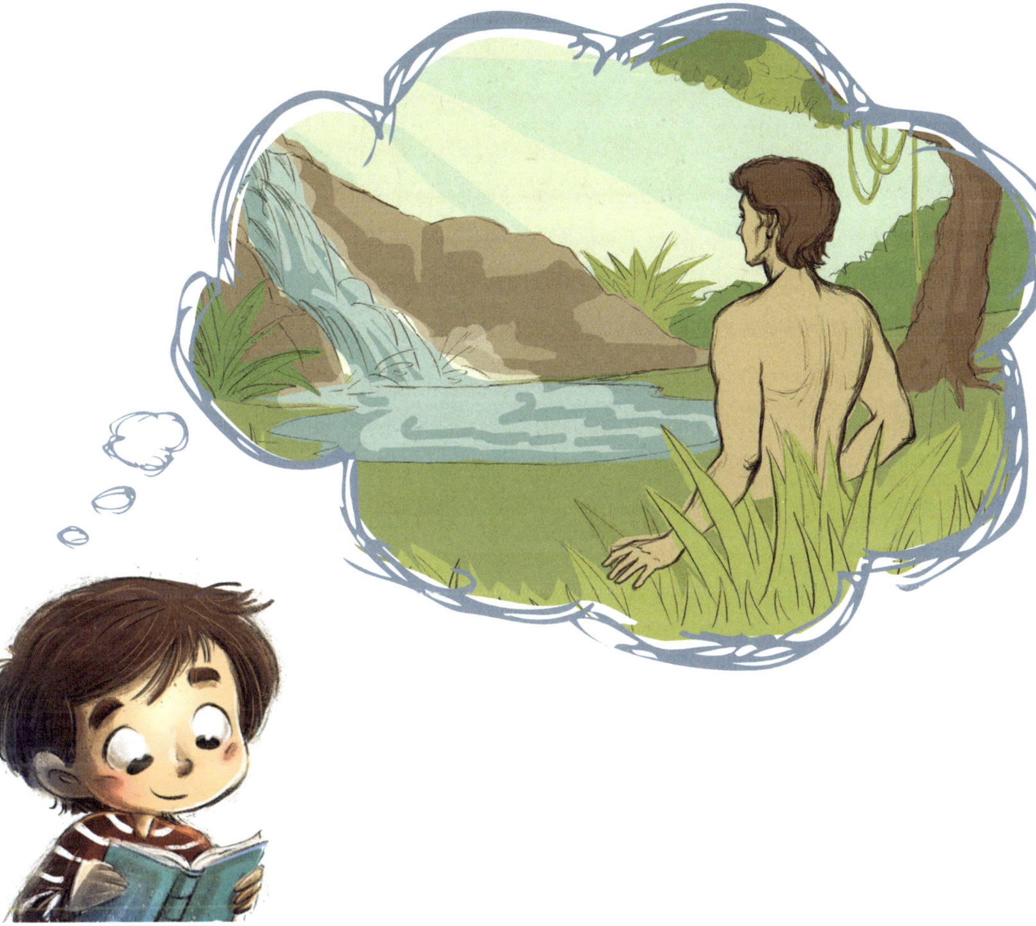

Prayer

Dear God, thank You for making us all special. Thank You especially for making my child and for making him/her perfect for our family. Amen.

God Makes the Garden

Then the LORD God planted a garden in the east, in a place called Eden, and put the man He had formed into it. **GENESIS 2:8**

God loved the people He had made very much, so He wanted to care for them. He made a beautiful garden for them to live in. In the garden there were rivers to drink from, trees to climb and pick fruit from, leaves to protect them from the hot sun, and a soft ground to sleep on at night.

Have your child draw a picture of a garden while you read Genesis 2:8-15 or the paraphrase above. Discuss all the things that God has given to you. **ASK:** Why do you think God wants to take care of us?

Cup your hands together and pretend you are holding an egg. Talk about how chickens lay them so we can have food. **ASK:** What other kinds of food do we eat? Where does it come from? What is your favorite thing to eat?

SAY: God gave Adam and Eve a home, and He gives us a home too. Walk through your home and thank God for each part of it—the roof, the floor, the walls, the windows, the beds, etc. Pray for children who don't have a home.

Turn on the water tap. **SAY:** Clean water is so easy to find! But did you know that in lots of countries, children have to go collect water in a bucket from a well or lake before they can drink or take a bath? Thank God for indoor plumbing, and pray for children who need clean water.

We know that God provides for us, and He also uses us to help provide for other people. Go through some of your things and choose a few items (food, toys, etc.) to give to someone in need.

Prayer

Dear God, thank You for all that You've provided for our family. Thank You specifically for...(create a list with your child of all the things God has provided for your family). Amen.

God Takes a Rest

By the seventh day God finished the work He had been doing, so He rested from all His work. **GENESIS 2:2**

God made the world and everything in it. That must have been a lot of work! So after working hard for six days, God took a day off. The Bible says that He "rested." God gives us times of rest too and created us to need it.

Read the paraphrase or Genesis 2:1-3. **ASK:** If you were God, what would you do on your day of rest? (Maybe He naps with a blanket made of stars or swings from a rainbow or sits on His throne and watches His favorite animals!)

Lay down with your child. **SAY:** God took a rest after creating everything, and He made us with the need to rest as well. That's why we sleep! (It might help a sleep-fighting preschooler to know that even God took a rest!) **ASK:** Why do you think God made our bodies to need sleep? What do you think might happen if we never went to sleep?

Clean up your child's room together. Afterward, take a break by resting. **ASK:** Why do you think God decided He needed a rest?

SAY: Resting was God's idea! What helps you relax? What makes you feel happy and peaceful?

Usually when we sleep, we dream. **ASK:** Can you remember any of your dreams? Sometimes we have bad dreams that scare us. Let's ask God to help us rest in peace tonight.

Prayer

Thank You, God, for all the wonderful things You created but also for taking a rest. Teach us how to rest well, knowing that we can sleep and rest because You are caring for us. Amen.

People Mess It Up

The woman saw that the tree was beautiful, that its fruit was good to eat, and that it would make her wise. So she took some of its fruit and ate it. She also gave some of the fruit to her husband who was with her, and he ate it. **GENESIS 3:6**

Adam and Eve, the first people on earth, loved being with God in their wonderful garden. But one day, something terrible happened. God had given Adam and Eve only one rule, and they broke the rule. And what happens when you break a rule? You get a consequence*. Adam and Eve's consequence was that they didn't get to be with God in their wonderful garden anymore.

**For kids who don't know the word "consequence," use the word "discipline" or "time-out" instead.*

Read the paraphrase or Genesis 3:1-6. **SAY:** Adam and Eve broke God's rule and disobeyed God. That's called "sin." **ASK:** Why do you think God gives us rules?

SAY: When we do something bad, we sin too, just like Adam and Eve. **ASK:** When is a time you've sinned? Have you ever broken a rule or not obeyed Mommy? Let's tell God about our sin. That is called "confession."

SAY: The Bible says that when Adam and Eve disobeyed, they tried to hide from God. Let's play hide-and-seek! (Play as long or short a time as you like.) **SAY:** Just like I can always find you when you hide, God found Adam and Eve too.

Grab some clothes from a drawer or laundry bin. **SAY:** Before Adam and Eve sinned, they didn't wear any clothes, and nobody cared! But after they sinned, they felt bad about being naked, so they wanted to wear clothes. God was kind and made them clothes. **ASK:** What kind of clothes do you like to wear?

SAY: We've talked about sin this week. Sin is sad because it pulls us away from God. But guess what? God made a way to fix our sin so we can be with Him again. He sent Jesus! The whole rest of the Bible is about God fixing our sin so we can be with him. Let's say THANK YOU as loud as we can!

Prayer

God, You are a perfect God, and we are not perfect people. We sin a lot. Thank You for sending Jesus to make a way for us to be with You forever. Amen.

God Gives Noah a Job

But I will make an agreement with you—you, your sons, your wife, and your sons' wives will all go into the boat. **GENESIS 6:18**

Sin grew and grew in people's hearts, and they hurt each other all the time. God had a plan to wash the sin from the earth, but He wanted to save someone very special. That special person was named Noah. Noah loved God, so God told him that in order to be saved from the big washing, he would have to build a boat. But this would not be a motorboat or a sailboat. This boat was to be made of wood and big enough to hold two of every kind of animal on the earth. Noah didn't even see any water around him, but he obeyed God, because he knew that God keeps His promises.

Read the paraphrase. Then **SAY:** The Bible says God told Noah how to build the ark. Let's use our imaginations and see if we can think of how God might have done that. **ASK:** Do you think God's voice boomed from heaven? Do you think He came and stood in front of Noah? Did God talk to him while Noah was dreaming? How do you think God talked to Noah? Let's be like Noah and obey God by building an ark. (Pretend to use a hammer and saw to build a big boat!)

ASK: Do you know why God wanted Noah to build a boat for saving his family and the animals? What was God going to do to the earth? Why do you think He wanted to do that? Remind your child that, while God wanted to get rid of all the badness on the earth once, He promised He would never wash the whole earth again.

SAY: Yesterday we talked about how God wanted to wash the earth clean and start over. **ASK:** Why do you think He saved Noah? (See Genesis 7:1 for the answer.) If you were going to wash the earth clean, who would you want to save?

SAY: One of the things that God did was send two of every kind of animal to the ark. Let's pretend to be some of those animals now! We need a boy lion/monkey/snake/mosquito and a girl lion/monkey/snake/mosquito. Let's go to the ark!

SAY: After Noah built the ark and God sent all the animals, God shut the door of the ark then sent a huge storm. Let's pretend we're on the ark in the middle of the biggest storm ever. (Rock back and forth, take care of the animals, and act a little seasick.) **ASK:** What do you think Noah and his family thought about when they were getting ready for the longest storm ever? Will God keep His promise to keep Noah safe?

Prayer

Thank You, God, for Your promise to love and protect us. Thanks for keeping Your promises to Noah and for bringing the animals to the ark and protecting them during the flood. Help us to trust and obey You like Noah did. Amen.

God Saves Noah

But God remembered Noah and all the wild and tame animals with him in the boat. He made a wind blow over the earth, and the water went down. **GENESIS 8:1**

After Noah's family and the animals climbed into the ark, God closed the door of the giant boat. Then He made it rain and rain and rain for forty days and forty nights. Then, Noah and his family and the animals waited in the ark for almost a year before the water went away. That's like waiting from one birthday all the way to the next birthday. What a long time to live on a boat! Finally, the ground was dry again. After they got off the ark, God promised Noah that He would never wash the whole earth again. God put the rainbow in the sky as a reminder of His promise.

Read the paraphrase, then make a big noisy storm together! Slap your knees to make rain, crash and boom to make thunder, and flicker the lights to make lightning. **ASK:** What does this story show us about God?

Help your child draw a picture of something that makes them afraid. Did you know that God is always with you, just like He was with Noah on the ark?

Read Noah's story from a children's Bible. **ASK:** What is your favorite part of the story? Why?

Look at the back of a CD or DVD to see if you can find the rainbow reflection. **ASK:** Do you see the rainbow? Why did God put a rainbow in the sky? Have you ever seen a rainbow outside?

Look around the room and find things in the colors of the rainbow. Thank God for putting the rainbow in the sky to remind us that He keeps His promises!

Prayer

Thank You, God, for protecting Noah in the ark and for giving us Your promises. We know You always keep Your promises. Amen.

God Chooses Abraham and Sarah

The LORD said to Abram, "Leave your country, your relatives, and your father's family, and go to the land I will show you." **GENESIS 12:1**

After the big flood, Noah's family grew and grew until there were lots of people on earth again. Remember how God wanted to fix our sin so people could be close to Him again? Well, His plan was going to take a long time. God picked Abraham and Sarah to be the first part of the plan. All they had to do was have a family! The problem was, Abraham and Sarah were both way too old to have babies. But nothing is impossible for God.

Read Genesis 12:1-3 or the paraphrase, ideally while under a make-shift tent or fort. **SAY:** God told Abraham to move to a new home. He promised that the whole world would be blessed because of Abraham. Let's pretend we're Abraham and pack up our tent! Abraham went where God told him to go! Walk around the house, pretending to be Abraham.

SAY: Abraham and Sarah lived for many years in the new land God gave them, but they still didn't have any babies. They were waiting for God's promise. **ASK:** It can be really hard to wait, right? What are you waiting for right now? How do you know it will come? How did Abraham and Sarah know God would keep His promise to them?

Read Genesis 15:5-6 while your child draws stars. **ASK:** How many stars did you draw? How many stars do you think are in the sky? God promised that Abraham would have even more people in his family! What does this story show us about God?

SAY: When Abraham was 99 years old, God told him he would have a baby next year. Sarah heard about this and laughed. Why do you think she laughed? Guess how old Abraham and Sarah were when they finally had their baby? (ages 100 and 90) They had to wait so long for their baby, but God definitely kept His promise!

SAY: We read about God's promises this week. Which ones can you remember? Practice saying Psalm 145:13 together: "The LORD will keep all his promises." Try saying it while looking through an imaginary telescope at the stars or while pretending to rock a baby in your arms.

Prayer

Thank You, God, for always keeping Your promises, especially Your promise to fix our sin problem. Help us to trust You and Your promises. Amen.

God Protects Joseph

Since Joseph was born when his father Israel was old, Israel loved him more than his other sons. **GENESIS 37:3**

Joseph's brothers didn't like him very much because he was his dad's favorite. God gave him dreams at night that showed he would be their boss someday. They were jealous of him and wanted to hurt him. One day they stole Joseph's clothes, beat him up, and threw him in a big hole! But God was with Joseph in the hole. Then, his brothers sold Joseph as a slave! But even as a slave in Egypt, God was with Joseph. He had many adventures as a slave, and even had to spend some time in jail, but even there, when he was all alone, God was with Joseph.

After reading the paraphrase to your kids, act out the events of Joseph's story together. **ASK:** Why do you think God let all this bad stuff happen to Joseph?

SAY: Joseph's brothers did these horrible things because they were jealous of and mad at Joseph. Have you ever gotten really mad at someone? What did you do? What do you think God wants us to do when we get angry? Let's talk to God about our anger right now.

Read Genesis 37:23-36 while your child draws a picture of Joseph's fancy coat. If your child has questions about all the bad things that happen to Joseph, remind them that God was with Joseph, even in this, and that God had a plan for Joseph's life.

Use this little experiment to teach your child what jealousy is. Find an item your child likes—perhaps a candy, a favorite blankie, or anything else that will entice your child. Show them the item then, very deliberately, keep it for yourself. Really ham it up so your child experiences the emotions. **SAY:** This is mine. Oh I love it so much. I'm so glad I have it. **SAY:** Tell me how you're feeling right now. I think you're feeling jealous. It's not a nice feeling, is it? That's how Joseph's brothers felt. They were jealous Joseph got fancy new clothes and didn't give any to them. When we feel jealous, we need to talk to God about our feelings and let Him help us do the right thing.

ASK: How do you think Joseph felt when he was all alone in that pit? How about when he was sold to be a slave? How about when he got sent to jail even though he didn't do anything wrong? One thing that Joseph knew was that God was with him. Let's practice memorizing a verse together: "I will be with you always" (Matthew 28:20).

Prayer

Thank You God for being in all those sad and lonely places with Joseph. Thank You for showing him that You were working out his life for the good. Help us to trust that You are always with us as well, even when life is hard. Amen.

God Helps Joseph Forgive

It was not you who sent me here, but God. **GENESIS 45:8**

While Joseph was in jail, Pharaoh had a very strange dream. God showed Joseph the meaning of Pharaoh's dream, and Pharaoh was so happy that he put Joseph in charge of the whole country. After a few years, no food could grow anywhere. People became very hungry. But because God helped Joseph plan ahead, there was food in Egypt. Even Joseph's brothers finally had to come to Egypt to ask for some food. When they got there, it was a big surprise to everyone that Joseph was in charge of Egypt. Joseph told them who he was, and God helped him forgive them for selling him as a slave.

After reading the paraphrase to your kids, act this story out together with them. **ASK:** Why do you think Joseph was able to forgive his older brothers?

SAY: God was with Joseph when he was in charge of the country. God helped him to do this very hard thing. **ASK:** Have you ever had to do something that was hard for you? (e.g., go to a day camp alone, do a chore that was difficult, or be kind to a sibling) Did you know that God promises to always be with you, no matter what hard things you have to do? Let's ask God to help us remember that!

Read the story of Joseph from a children's Bible while your child draws a picture of Joseph and his brothers.

SAY: Joseph's brothers had to travel all the way from their country to Egypt just to get some food. How do you think they felt when they got there? How do you feel when you're really hungry? Let's pretend that we're really hungry. (rub your tummy and groan) I'm so glad that God had a plan for how He was going to feed Joseph's brothers. He used their terrible plan to hurt Joseph to get Joseph into Egypt and to get him in charge of the country and to save food so that Joseph's brothers could come buy some and be saved! Sometimes God does some pretty strange and amazing things.

You will need a piece of paper, a crayon/marker, and a band-aid. Draw a heart on the paper. **SAY:** Sometimes people hurt us, just like Joseph's brothers hurt him. Can you think of a time when someone hurt you? When your child has an answer, write it down in the heart, then draw a jagged line through the heart to make it look broken. **SAY:** When people hurt us, it can feel like our heart is broken. Sometimes they do it on purpose and sometimes they don't even know that our heart is hurt. But God wants us to forgive them. The only way to really heal this broken heart is for us to forgive that person. Forgiving someone means that we stop being mad at them. Can you stop being mad at the person who hurt you? Let's put a band-aid on that heart to show our forgiveness. Sometimes forgiveness is really hard, but we can ask God to help us.

Prayer

Help us to forgive like Joseph did. We know it wasn't easy for him to forgive his brothers, but thank You for helping him to do it. May we always remember to ask You for help when we can't stop being mad at someone. Amen.

God Saves Baby Moses

She put the baby in the basket. Then she put the basket among the tall stalks of grass at the edge of the Nile River. **EXODUS 2:3**

Joseph's whole family came to live in Egypt, and God's family grew and grew. After many years, the new king of Egypt hated God's people, the Israelites. He made a law that every Israelite baby boy was supposed to be thrown into the river. But one mommy got really brave and smart, and she put her son in a basket in the river. Soon, a princess came by, and she found the baby. She decided to adopt him, so this baby ended up living in the palace with the Pharaoh. This baby's name was Moses. God had great plans for Moses later in his life, so He protected him while he was a baby.

Read the paraphrase to your child, then act out the story together, using a stuffed toy or a doll as Moses. (Or your child can pretend to be baby Moses if they like to be silly!) **ASK:** Why do you think God wanted Moses to grow up in the palace?

SAY: God protected baby Moses. Is there anyone in your life that could use God's protection right now? Maybe you have a friend that's sick or maybe you're just learning how to ride a bike, and you keep hurting yourself. Maybe your mom is going to have a baby or your grandpa is going on a long trip. Who should we pray for today?

Take care of a baby doll together (or stuffed animal). **ASK:** How do parents take care of their babies? Let's do some of those things for this baby. God gave Moses' mommy the idea to keep him safe in a very unusual way!

Read the story right from the Bible (Exodus 1:22-2:10) or from a picture Bible while your child draws a picture of a basket.

SAY: God uses other people to take care of us, just like He used Miriam and the princess to take care of Moses. **ASK:** Who takes care of you? How do they take care of you?

Prayer

God, thank You for protecting baby Moses. Please protect me, because I know You have plans for me too! Amen.

God Speaks to Moses

When the LORD saw Moses was coming to look at the bush, God called to him from the bush, "Moses, Moses!" And Moses said, "Here I am." **EXODUS 3:4**

When Moses grew up, he left Egypt and became a shepherd in the desert. One day, he saw something strange—a bush that was on fire but didn't burn up. Then the bush got even more weird—it started to talk! It was God talking to him. Moses was very scared, but God told him that He had chosen Moses to go set the Israelites free from Pharaoh and the Egyptians. Moses' special job was to go ask Pharaoh to let all his people go free. Moses was even more scared when he heard this! But God gave him courage, and Moses obeyed God.

Read the paraphrase then act out the story with your child. If you don't like to act, use stuffed animals and help your child reenact the story that way. **ASK:** Why do you think God spoke through a burning bush?

SAY: Even though Moses knew that God is great and very powerful, he was still scared to talk to the mean Pharaoh. Are there any things God could help you not be scared about? Maybe you are kind of scared of preschool or your babysitter, or maybe you're scared of the dark. Let's talk to God about that right now.

Read the story right from the Bible (Exodus 3:1-10 and 4:1-17) or from a children's Bible while your child draws a picture of a fire.

SAY: God asked Moses to take off his sandals because he was standing on holy ground, which meant that he was standing close to God. It also says that Moses covered his face because he was afraid to look at God. We don't have to be afraid to talk to God, but let's take off our shoes and socks now, and pray that God would stand close to us! We can cover our faces too and pretend to be like Moses if you like.

SAY: God told Moses what to do, and he (eventually) did it. Do you think it was easy for Moses to do what God asked? Why did he do it anyway? Let's practice our obeying right now with a fun little game. Play "Simon Says" with your child.

Prayer

God, thank You for seeing the needs of Your people and sending someone to help them. Help me to listen and obey too when You give me a job. Amen

God Shows His Power through Plagues

"I will punish Egypt with my power, and I will bring the Israelites out of that land. Then they will know I am the LORD." **EXODUS 7:5**

Moses asked Pharaoh to let the Israelites go free, but Pharaoh said "NO." God showed his amazing power to Pharaoh by making lots of wild things happen to the Egyptians, called "plagues." He made millions of frogs and bugs come into their houses and even be in their food! Then He made everyone get really sick and all kinds of other bad things to happen. God did this because He wanted Pharaoh to find out how great and powerful God is. But after each plague was gone, Moses would ask Pharaoh to let the people go, and each time Pharaoh said "NO!" Finally, plague number ten made Pharaoh really sad and he told Moses to take the Israelites and leave.

Act out the story with your child or read the paraphrase. Use as many plagues in your story as you like in your re-enactment. Here is a list: water turns to blood; frogs; gnats/lice; flies; sick animals; sores on the skin; hail; locusts; darkness; death of the firstborn. **ASK:** Why did God send the plagues? What does this story show us about God?

SAY: God made all those bad things happen to Pharaoh and his people because He was teaching them about His power. Are there any bad things that are happening in your life right now? Maybe somebody is sick or you have to move or your family gets mad at each other a lot. Think of something, then pray together, inviting God to show His power.

One of the plagues was bugs EVERYWHERE. Pretend to be like bugs and hop/fly around everywhere. **ASK:** How do you think the people of Egypt liked this plague? Pretty gross, isn't it? Why do you think Pharaoh kept changing his mind even when God kept sending terrible plagues on his people?

SAY: To be saved from the very last plague, each Israelite family had to kill a lamb and put its blood on their doorposts. It seems really sad, but the blood of the this lamb protected their children from death. Pretend to paint the lamb's blood on your doorposts, then **SAY:** Thank you God for making a way to save the children from death. (If your kids are older, you can point to Jesus here, telling your kids that Jesus is the final Passover lamb who saves us all from death.)

SAY: Pharaoh learned that God is great and very powerful. The best part was that the Israelites didn't have to be slaves anymore! Memorize the following Bible verse together while pretending to be a frog. "Our Lord is great and very powerful!" Psalm 147:5

Prayer

God, You are great and very powerful. Thank You for showing Pharaoh, the Israelites, and Moses how amazing and powerful You are. Amen.

God Opens the Red Sea

"I will make the king stubborn again so he will chase after them, but I will defeat the king and his army. This will bring honor to me, and the Egyptians will know that I am the LORD." **EXODUS 14:4**

God's people left Egypt and started walking to the Promised Land, but they got stuck at the edge of the Red Sea. Suddenly, Pharaoh decided he didn't want to let them go after all. He gathered all his soldiers with their swords, horses, and chariots, and they started chasing God's people to try to get them back. The Israelites were very, very afraid, but God protected them. He sent a big wind to do something amazing—it blew the sea wide open so the people could walk across the Red Sea on a dry path! Then, when Pharaoh's army tried to chase the Israelites, God made the water crash back down so they couldn't catch God's people anymore. They were finally free!

Read the paraphrase then act out the story. **ASK:** What does this story show us about God?

Get a bowl of water, fill up a sink with water, or fill a bathtub. Ask your child to blow really hard and try to make a path in the middle of the water. **SAY:** Can you do it? Who is the only one who can do such an amazing miracle? Why did He do that miracle?

Read the story right from the Bible (Exodus 14:1-29) or from a picture Bible while your child draws a picture of the sea.

SAY: Moses and his people were really, really scared, but God helped them to be brave. Do you know anyone who is brave? Let's see if we can think of some brave people around us. Or maybe even a time when you have been brave. (Talk about Daddy driving carefully in a storm or Mommy starting a new job. Perhaps your child is taking swimming lessons and being brave even when they go under water.) Pray about whatever comes up in the conversation.

SAY: Yesterday we said that Moses and his people were brave to walk right through the Red Sea. Do you know WHY Moses was brave? Because he knew that God was with him, and God could protect him. Do you know why you can be brave? Because God is with you too! And He can protect you.

Prayer

Thank You, God, for protecting the Israelites and saving them from their enemies! Thank You for reminding me of Your power. Help me to trust You everyday. Amen.

God Leads His People

The LORD showed them the way; during the day he went ahead of them in a pillar of cloud, and during the night he was in a pillar of fire to give them light. **EXODUS 13:21**

When God's people left Egypt, they didn't know where to go. Thankfully, God guided them by setting a big pillar of cloud before them in the daytime and changing it into a pillar of fire in the night. That way, the Israelites always knew that God was with them and that He would guide them. All they had to do was follow the pillar of cloud and fire!

Read the paraphrase then act out Israel's story with your child. **ASK:** Why do you think God chose to lead them this way?

SAY: God's people got to see that God was with them always, because they could always see the pillar of cloud or fire. We can't see God like that, but He is still with us! Let's draw pictures of some places where God is with us. Is God with us at home? Church? The grocery store? Swimming lessons? Preschool? Let's thank God for being with us in those places!

Read the story right from the Bible (Exodus 13:21-22) while your child draws a picture of a cloud or fire.

Look at a map together. (on a computer, phone, or an actual paper map) **SAY:** God's people didn't have a map to follow to the Promised Land. Instead, they had to just trust that God would take them the right way. We don't have a pillar of cloud or fire to follow, but what are some ways that we can learn to follow God in our lives?

Play "follow the leader" and remind your child that the Israelites had to follow the pillars of cloud and fire, because that was God's way of showing them where to go!

Prayer

Thank You, God, for promising to be with us and guide us. Help us to follow You always! Amen.

God Provides for the Israelites

Then the LORD said to Moses, "I will cause food to fall like rain from the sky for all of you." **EXODUS 16:4**

The Israelites were finally safe from the mean Pharaoh, but now they were stuck in the desert where there was no food or water! They whined and complained to Moses because their tummies were so hungry and their bodies were so thirsty. Moses talked to God about it, and God sent them food in a very strange way. When the people woke up in the morning, there was a strange kind of bread all over the ground. They called it "manna." At night there was meat on the ground for them to gather and eat. God also made water pour out of a rock for them to drink.

Read the paraphrase, then act out the story with your child, using yourselves as characters. Feel free to ham it up with lots of complaining about the living conditions! **ASK:** Why do you think God took care of such complainers? What does this story show us about God?

Pretend to hold a heavy rock (or if you have one around, hold a real one). Try to drink from it. **SAY:** Mmmm, what tasty water this is. What? This isn't a glass of water? Well, what is it? A rock? Oh dear, but I'm really thirsty! Hey, do you remember that story from the Bible about how God made water come from a rock? Do you think I could do that? Nope, only God can. Why did He do that? (they were in the desert, there was no water to drink, He cared for them) Does God care for you too?

Take a field trip to the kitchen to check out the contents of your fridge/cupboards/freezer. **ASK:** What kinds of food do we have? What kind of food did God give to the Israelites in the desert? Isn't our God so great and powerful?

Read the story right from the Bible (Exodus 16:4-18, 31, and/or 17:1-6) or from a children's Bible while your child draws a picture of their favorite food.

ASK: What is your favorite part of this Bible story? What type of food do you think you would have liked the best? (crackers or meat) What would you think if there were crackers all over the grass outside when you woke up tomorrow morning?

Prayer

God, thank You for giving the Israelites something to eat and drink even though they were cranky grumblers. Help us to remember that we can trust You with all of our needs because You are great and very powerful! Amen.

God's Rules

"So now if you obey me and keep My agreement, you will be My own possession, chosen from all nations." **EXODUS 19:5**

In the desert, God told Moses that He would visit the people in a cloud. But this was not just any cloud: it was a huge, ginormous cloud that covered a whole mountain! The mountain was covered in smoke and lightning because God came down on the mountain in a fire. The mountain shook, and the sound of trumpets grew louder and louder. The people were terrified with a capital *T*! In the middle of the noise and smoke, God called to Moses to climb up the mountain. Moses did, and while he was there, God gave him ten rules. When he came down, Moses was in charge of teaching the rules to the people.

This week we're going to summarize some of the rules. Make sure to read the paraphrase, and feel free to share the other rules with your child if you feel they need to hear one of the ones that weren't covered.

SAY: The most important rule to remember is that God is the most important. He's #1! Why do you think God wants to be the most important? What kind of things can get in the way of God being #1? How can we make sure God is always #1 in our lives? Pray together, asking God to help you make Him #1 in your lives.

SAY: Another one of God's rules is that we are supposed to love and obey our mommies and daddies. What are some ways you can do that? Ask God to help you and your child honor your/their parents.

SAY: Another one of God's rules is that we shouldn't want what others have or try to take what others have. This is a really hard one, isn't it? Can you think of a time when you wanted something that someone else had? Can you think of a time when you took something that wasn't yours? Pray together, asking God to help you to be content with what you have and to help you to try not to take things that aren't yours.

SAY: God also wants us to be truthful. What does that mean? Pray about it together, asking God to help you and your child be truthful.

SAY: Another of God's most important rules is that we should love others instead of hurting them. How can we do that today? Pray about it together!

Prayer

Thank You, God, for Your rules, and that You give them to us because You love us. Help us to love and obey You and to accept Your forgiveness when we mess up. Amen.

God Saves Rahab

So the men went to Jericho and stayed at the house of a prostitute named Rahab. **JOSHUA 2:1**

God's people were finally ready to get out of the desert and into the Promised Land. The problem was, there were people already living there. The new leader, Joshua, sent two spies to check out the city of Jericho. There were some bad guys who wanted to catch the spies, so a lady named Rahab hid them on her roof. She knew God and knew the Israelites were going to take over her city, so she asked the spies to save her and her family. They promised that if she kept a red rope hanging from her window, they would be able to save her. So they climbed out of the city down the red rope in the middle of the night and ran back to Joshua. Later, when the walls of Jericho came tumbling down, the spies found Rahab and her family and saved them.

Act out the story with your child, using yourselves as characters. (Or just read the paraphrased story with gusto!) **ASK:** Why do you think God chose to save Rahab? What does this story show us about God?

Grab something red—a ribbon, a pair of pants, a belt, a shirt—anything long and skinny will do. **SAY:** The Bible says that Rahab knew all the things that God had done for the Israelites when they were in the desert (like opening up the Red Sea) and that she believed in God because of those things. Tie your red item somewhere your child will see it (doorknob, bed frame). **ASK:** Just like Rahab, we can know about the things that God has done, and we can believe in God because of those things. Let's let this red item remind us of how God saved Rahab and the spies.

Option 1: Play a short game of hide and seek with your child.
Option 2: Hide under a blanket together while you discuss the story. **ASK:** Do you think the spies were scared when the bad guys came to where they were hiding? Where would you hide from a bad guy? I'm so glad that God protected the spies, and God protects you too!

Read the story right from the Bible (Joshua 2:1-22, 6:23) or from a picture Bible while your child draws a picture of a red rope.

Pretend to be spies together. Skulk around your house, sneaking around corners and using silly hand gestures. **ASK:** What do you see? Are there any bad guys around? What would you look for if you were looking for a new place to live?Why do you think God protected the spies?

Prayer

God, You are great and very powerful. Thank You for protecting the spies from the bad guys and for saving Rahab and her family. Amen.

God Defeats Jericho

At the sound of the trumpets and the people's shout, the walls fell, and everyone ran straight into the city. **JOSHUA 6:20**

God's people were ready to take over the city of Jericho. They didn't know how to get in because there were REALLY big rock walls around the city, but God gave His people a strange plan. They marched around the city once a day for six days. Then, on the seventh day, they walked around the city seven whole times. The last time they walked around, the people made as much noise as they could—they screamed and shouted and blasted their trumpets super loud. The walls began to crack, and then the walls began to crumble, and then the big, thick, sturdy rock walls came crashing down! God's people climbed over the fallen walls and took over the city.

Read the paraphrase then act out the story of Israel's victory with your child. **ASK:** Why do you think God gave His people such strange directions?

Look out a window with your child and pretend that you see an army of people marching around your house. **ASK:** What would you think about that? Would you be scared or maybe think the people were being a little silly?

ASK: What would you have done to knock down the walls of a city? What do you think of God's plan for taking over Jericho? Sometimes God's plans don't make any sense to us, but when we trust Him, we discover that He does some pretty amazing things! Can you think of some other amazing things that God has done?

Read the story right from the Bible (Joshua 6:6-20) or from a children's Bible while your child draws a picture of a pile of rocks.

Pretend to toot a horn, then practice memorizing Psalm 147:5: "Our Lord is great and very powerful!"

Prayer

Thank You God for knocking down the walls of Jericho! Help us to trust You to do amazing things in our lives too. Amen.

God Defeats the Midianites

Gideon went back to the camp of Israel and called out to them, "Get up! The LORD has handed the army of Midian over to you!" **JUDGES 7:15**

At a time when God's people were finally living in the Promised Land, there was a big bad army who wanted to hurt God's people! God asked Gideon to get an army ready to fight them. Lots of people signed up to fight the bad guys, but God wanted to have a teeny tiny army instead. So Gideon sent some of the people home. Then Gideon took his teeny tiny army and gave them each a trumpet and a light inside a jar. They surrounded the big bad army in the middle of the night and gave them a big scare; they blew their trumpets and smashed their jars, and God made the big bad army so afraid they started fighting with each other instead of with Gideon's army. The rest of them ran away and God's people were saved.

Read the paraphrase then act out the story with your child. Use stuffed animals or dolls for the army. **ASK:** Why do you think God wanted such a tiny army?

Practice memorizing Proverbs 3:5 together: "Trust the Lord with all your heart." Try saying it like a big scary army and like a teeny tiny army. **ASK:** How did Gideon have to trust God? What can you trust God about?

SAY: The people in the big bad army were called Midianites, and they were really mean to God's people. Have you ever met someone that wasn't very kind to you? If so, let's talk to God about that person and ask Him to help us trust in Him with all our hearts.

Either use your imagination to pretend you have a flashlight or get a real one for this activity. Pretend that you are in Gideon's army. Sneak around your house and get to a dark place (like a bathroom) then blow your pretend trumpets, turn on your lights or the flashlight, and shout "for the Lord and for Gideon!" like his army did.

Have your child draw a picture of a trumpet or a light while you read the story from the Bible (Judges 7:1-22) or from a picture Bible.

Prayer

Thank You, Lord, for showing Gideon and his army they could trust You to win the battle, even with a teeny tiny army! You really are great and powerful, God. Amen.

God Gives Naomi a Family

But Ruth said, "Don't beg me to leave you or to stop following you. Where you go, I will go. Where you live, I will live. Your people will be my people, and your God will be my God." **RUTH 1:16**

Naomi and her family moved away from the town of Bethlehem because there was no food to eat. They walked all the way to the country of Moab. A long time later, Naomi's husband and two sons got sick and died. The only family she had left were the women who had been married to her sons. She was very sad, so she decided to go back home. Naomi told the women they should stay in Moab. One of them, Ruth, decided to stay with Naomi. Ruth left the country that she knew, the family that she grew up with, and the friends that she loved, and went with Naomi back to Bethlehem. They didn't know where they would live or what they would eat, but they did have each other. When they got back to Bethlehem, Ruth took care of Naomi by picking barley from the fields for them to eat.

Read the paraphrase then act out the story with your child. Be sure to walk a long way through your house! **ASK:** Why do you think God helped Ruth stay with Naomi?

Gather a bunch of similar small items (like scraps of paper or small toys). **SAY:** Ruth did something called "gleaning," which is when she picked up the leftover barley from someone else's field. God had a special rule that said farmers were supposed to leave the leftover barley for poor people to glean. Let's try gleaning. I will put some stuff on the floor, and we'll pick it up.

ASK: Who is in our family? What makes up a family? What does our family do to help one another? How did God use Ruth to help Naomi?

Have your child draw a picture of something from the story while you review it together. This passage is quite long to read straight out of the Bible (Ruth 1), but you may find a shorter version in a children's Bible.

ASK: How did Ruth show that she loved Naomi? How do you think Naomi felt when Ruth showed her this kind of love? Do you know where true love comes from? It comes from God, who is love.

Prayer

Thank You, God, for families. Help my family to be the best that it can be, and help us all to love You like You love us. Amen.

God Gives Ruth a Family

One day Ruth, the Moabite, said to Naomi, "I am going to the fields. Maybe someone will be kind enough to let me gather the grain he leaves behind." **RUTH 2:2**

Ruth went out to pick barley from a field so that she could feed herself and Naomi. The man who was in charge of the field noticed her. He thought she was very brave for coming back to Bethlehem with Naomi, and he told her that she could pick barley from his field every day. His name was Boaz. Later, Boaz and Ruth got married and had a baby. God gave Naomi and Ruth a new family.

Read the paraphrase then act out the story of Ruth with your child. **ASK:** Why do you think God chose to save Ruth and Naomi? What does this story show us about God?

Play Ring around the Rosy with the following words:
God's love is amazing / We're singing and we're praising
We love others / Because He first loved us.

SAY: Our story is about love—the love that Ruth had for Naomi, the love that Boaz and Ruth had for each other, and most of all, the love that God has for each one of us. We love others because God first loved us.

Show your children something made of grain. (cereal, bread, oat-meal, crackers, etc.) **ASK:** Why do you think Ruth went out to collect grain? Was there anywhere else she could get food? So how did Ruth take care of Naomi? How does God take care of you?

SAY: Ruth was a special part of Naomi's family, but she is also part of the family of Jesus! She was King David's great-grandma, and she was Jesus' great-great-and-many-more-greats-grandma. Help your child draw a picture of your family. Discuss each person then pray for each family member individually.

SAY: Ruth, Naomi, and Boaz lived in a town named Bethlehem. Can you think of some other people who lived in Bethlehem? (Both King David and Jesus were born in Bethlehem.)

Prayer

Thank You, God, for making a whole family out of a bunch of lonely people—Ruth, Naomi, and Boaz. Please help our family to love and praise You like this family did. Amen.

God Answers Hannah's Prayer

She made a promise, saying, "LORD All-Powerful, see how sad I am. Remember me and don't forget me." **1 SAMUEL 1:11**

Hannah loved God but was very sad because she had no children. One day she went to the tabernacle, God's special place to pray, and she asked God for a baby. She was praying so hard that she started crying, and a priest named Eli came to talk to her. He told her that God was going to answer her prayer, and He did! She had a baby named Samuel. When he was still a little boy, she brought him to the tabernacle to live and to serve the Lord with Eli.

Read the paraphrase then act out the story of Hannah with your child. **ASK:** Why do you think God chose to answer Hannah's prayer? What does this story show us about God?

SAY: Hannah gave her son to God because she was so happy that God had answered her prayer for a baby. Have you ever prayed for something and had God say yes? Is there something we can pray about now?

ASK: When he was still a kid, Samuel went to live in the tabernacle, which would be like you living at the church. **ASK:** How would you like to live at church with the pastor instead of at home with your family? What do you think would be fun about that? What would be sad about it?

Read this passage straight from the Bible (1 Samuel 1:9-28) while your child draws a picture of a baby.

SAY: God gives us all a family, just like He gave Hannah a family. Who is in our family? Talk about your immediate/extended family and then pray for them.

Prayer

Thank You for showing Hannah that she could trust You, even when she thought she would never have a baby. Thank You for baby Samuel and all the wonderful ways he served as he lived and worked in the tabernacle. Amen.

God Speaks to Samuel

The LORD came and stood there and called as He had before, "Samuel, Samuel!" **1 SAMUEL 3:10**

Samuel was a boy who lived in God's temple with Eli. One night, they were both asleep when someone called "Samuel!" Samuel ran over to Eli and said "Here I am! Did you call me?" Eli was confused because he hadn't called Samuel. He told him to go back to bed. Then Samuel heard his name called again. So again, Samuel jumped up and ran to Eli to help, but Eli hadn't called him. Samuel went back to bed and it happened again! Finally, Eli figured out that it was God who was calling Samuel, so he told Samuel to speak to God the next time he called. Samuel went back to bed, and God called him again, "Samuel! Samuel!" This time, Samuel said "Speak, your servant is listening," and God spoke to Samuel.

Read the paraphrase then act out the story together. **ASK:** Why do you think God spoke to Samuel in the middle of the night? What does this story show us about God?

ASK: If you heard your name in the middle of the night, what would you do? Would you think it was me? What do you think God's voice sounds like?

Have your child lay in bed and close their eyes. Whisper their name, then have them practice saying "Talk to me, God! I am listening!"

Read the story straight from the Bible (1 Samuel 3:1-10) while your child draws a picture of Samuel sleeping.

SAY: Samuel listened to God! Let's practice our listening skills by playing Simon Says. Have your child do various activities, using your own ideas so they can be an appropriate age and energy level.

Prayer

Thank You, God, for speaking to Samuel and for speaking to us through the Bible. Please help us to listen to You too, whether it's while we're sleeping, when we're awake, or wherever we are. Help us to listen and obey. Amen.

God Chooses a New King

"God does not see the same way people see. People look at the outside of a person, but the LORD looks at the heart." **1 SAMUEL 16:7**

God asked Samuel to pour oil on the head of the man who would be the next king. But Samuel didn't know who it was supposed to be! He went to pick one of the sons of a man named Jesse. He looked at the first tall, strong, and handsome man, and thought, this man would make a great king! But God told him that he was looking for someone who loved God. Finally, Samuel found David, who was just a shepherd boy. Nobody knew a shepherd boy could turn out to be a king, but God knew. Samuel poured oil on his head and told him that someday, he would be king of the whole country.

Read the story paraphrase together then act it out using yourselves or stuffed animals as characters. **ASK:** Do you think Samuel thought it was weird that the little shepherd boy was going to be the king? What does this story show us about God?

SAY: When Samuel was looking for the king there were seven men that stood in front of him. Let's look at them all. Man #1 (point up with one finger), are you the kind of king God wants? Nope. Ok, man #2, are you the kind of king God wants? Ok, man #7, are YOU the kind of king God wants? NO?! Then who's left? Oh, this smelly little shepherd boy. Hm. Ok, boy #1, are YOU the kind of king that God wants? Oh, God says YES! I'm so glad that God has a plan.

Interactive option: pretend to be a patient while the doctor takes an X-ray of your heart! **SAY:** Many times when we go to the doctor, he can't tell if we have something wrong just by looking at us. We may look just fine on the outside, but there might be something wrong on the inside. To see what is on the inside, the doctor uses machines like X-rays and ultrasound. By looking with the machine, he can see what's on the inside and help us to get well. God does the same thing. He looks at our inside and wants us to have a heart that loves Him. What do you think is inside your heart?

ASK: What do you think a king does all day? Do you think it's a hard job? Do you think God helped David when it was his turn to be king? What kinds of hard jobs do you do that you could ask God to help you with?

Read the story right out of the Bible (1 Samuel 16:1-13) while your child draws a picture of a king's crown. **ASK:** Did you notice anything different about these Bible verses today?

Prayer

Thank You, God, for looking at who we really are, and not just looking at how strong we are or how good-looking we are. Help us to love You with all our hearts. Amen.

God Gives David Strength

"The LORD who saved me from a lion and a bear will save me from this Philistine." 1 SAMUEL 17:37

David was a shepherd. He cared for his sheep and wrote songs to God. David once told a story about what it was like to be a shepherd. He said that one time a big lion came roaring in and stole one of his sheep! He went after it, rescued the sheep, and killed the lion. A bear also tried to steal a sheep, but God helped David to protect his sheep from the bear too. David knew that God had helped him and protected him from the animals who wanted to hurt him and his sheep.

Read the story paraphrase together then act it out using yourselves or stuffed animals as characters. **ASK:** Do you think David was scared when the lion and bear came to steal his sheep? What does this story show us about God?

SAY: As a shepherd, the sheep followed David wherever he went. Let's play "follow the leader" and pretend to be David and his sheep.

SAY: David had a whole bunch of sheep to take care of. Do you have an animal that you take care of? How do you take care of it? How does God take care of the animals?

David learned how to be a good shepherd from God. The Bible says God is like our shepherd. Together with your child, pretend to be a shepherd and a sheep as you read the following excerpts from Psalm 23.

"The LORD is my shepherd, I have everything I need."
"He lets me rest in green pastures."
"He leads me to calm water."

ASK: How does God do these things for us?

As you read 1 Samuel 17:24-37, have your child draw their version of God being with them when they're scared. **SAY:** David knows that God will help him and protect him against a big giant because God had helped him and protected him against the lion and the bear. Where has God helped you or protected you?

Prayer

Thank You, God, for helping David take good care of his sheep! Please help me trust You when I am afraid. Amen.

God, David, and Goliath

But David said to him, "You come to me using a sword and two spears. But I come to you in the name of the LORD All-Powerful, the God of the armies of Israel!" **1 SAMUEL 17:45**

When Saul was king of Israel, there was a big bad enemy army with a big bad enemy soldier named Goliath. This big bad soldier made fun of God and God's people and tried to hurt them. David was angry that Goliath was making fun of God's people. He wanted everyone to know that God is the best and doesn't need a huge army to save people. So David picked up a stone and put it in his sling, then whipped the sling around over his head. When he let it go, the sling let loose the itty-bitty stone, which flew into the giant's big, mean, round head and knocked him down!

Find the biggest stuffed animal you have in the house and the smallest. Pretend they are David and Goliath and reenact the showdown. **ASK:** What did Goliath say to David? What did David say to Goliath? What does this story show us about God?

Find something small and soft, like a cotton ball or a small stuffed animal. Have your child throw it at you to see if they can knock you down. **ASK:** Why do you think you couldn't knock me down? How do you think David knocked down Goliath with just a small rock? Do you think he had help from someone?

Draw a picture of David and Goliath together while talking about the story. **SAY:** I wonder how Goliath felt when he saw that stone coming toward his face?

Practice memorizing the following verse while pretending to swing a sling. When you say "possible," let the pretend sling fly! "For God all things are possible" (Matthew 19:26).

SAY: There are lots of things in our lives that can seem really big and scary. Is there something that seems really scary to you right now? Something that you're afraid of? Read David's words in 1 Samuel 17:47. **ASK:** Who is the One who protects us? Let's ask God right now to save you from what is scaring you.

Prayer

Thank You, God, for helping David take down the big mean giant. You are bigger than any problem; help me to remember to ask You for help when I have questions or issues. Amen.

God Gives Us Friends

Jonathan made an agreement with David, because he loved David as much as himself. **1 SAMUEL 18:3**

Jonathan was a prince, and his dad was King Saul of Israel. There was a boy that King Saul really didn't like, and that boy's name was David. But guess who thought David was pretty cool? That's right, Prince Jonathan! Prince Jonathan wanted to be David's friend, so they made a promise to each other to love each other as friends. To show David that he was telling the truth, Prince Jonathan gave David some of his clothes, his bow and arrow, and his belt.

Read the paraphrase and/or act out the story of David and Jonathan's pact with your child. **ASK:** Why do you think God chose these two to be friends?

ASK: Who are the friends God has given you? What do you like to do with your friends? What do you do to show your friends that you love them?

ASK: What did Jonathon give to David to show that they were friends? Can you think of something you could give to one of your friends? Ask God to help you think of an idea!

Read 1 Samuel 18:3-4 from the Bible while your child draws a picture of them and a friend playing together.

Cut out (or tear) a few long strips of a piece of paper. Tape or staple them together to fit your child around the waist, like the belt that Jonathan gave to David. On it, write the following verse: "Be kind and loving to each other" (Ephesians 4:32).

Help your child put the belt on, then ask them about what it says on their belt. You can ask it in different ways or be silly and pretend that you keep forgetting. Before you know it, your child will have memorized the verse!

Prayer

Thank You, God, for friends. Help me to learn how to be a friend and to find good friends to be with me in my life. Amen.

God Cares for Elijah

The birds brought Elijah bread and meat every morning and evening, and he drank water from the stream. 1 KINGS 17:6

The king of Israel didn't love God and didn't like God's friend Elijah very much either. Elijah told the king God was going to punish him for disobeying by making it not rain for three years. This made the king super duper mad, so God told Elijah to go into hiding for a while. He camped out by a brook, and every day God sent ravens to feed him. The birds brought bread and meat for breakfast and supper every day.

Read the story paraphrase together or act it out using yourselves or some stuffed birds as characters. **SAY:** Why do you think God decided to feed Elijah this way?

SAY: Pretend to be a raven getting a message from God about bringing food to Elijah. What does God tell you? Where do you get the food from? How do you know where to find Elijah?

Read 1 Kings 17:1-6 while your child draws a picture of a bird and bread. **ASK:** Why do you think God sent food for Elijah?

SAY: 1 Kings 17:5 says Elijah did as the Lord had told him, even though God told him to go camp beside a brook for months. God was able to meet all of Elijah's needs because Elijah obeyed God. Pray together, asking God to meet your needs, and that you would be brave enough to obey whatever He asks.

Flap your wings like a raven and practice memorizing a verse! "My God will meet all your needs" (Philippians 4:19 NIV). **ASK:** How has God met your needs today?

Prayer

Thank You, God, for meeting the needs of Elijah and for giving him water and food and a safe place to stay. We trust You to meet our needs as well. Thank You! Amen.

God Saves a Hungry Widow

Then the LORD spoke his word to Elijah, "Go to Zarephath in Sidon and live there. I have commanded a widow there to take care of you." **1 KINGS 17:8-9**

Because there was no rain for a long time, the brook where Elijah was hiding dried up. God told him to go to a different town and live with a woman and her son. The lady didn't want to give Elijah any food, because she had only a tiny little bit left, and she was afraid she and her son would starve. Elijah said that if she shared with him, God promised her food would never run out. So she shared her food with him, and God saved the woman, her son, and Elijah from starvation.

Read the story paraphrase together and/or act it out using yourselves as characters! **ASK:** Why do you think God chose to save this widow instead of just feeding only Elijah?

SAY: Both the widow and Elijah showed obedience to God. Elijah went to the town, and the widow gave him bread. God was able to meet all of Elijah's needs and the widow's needs because they obeyed God. Pray together, asking God that He would meet your needs, and that you would be brave enough to obey whatever He asks.

Read the story of Elijah from 1 Kings 17:7-16 while your child draws a picture of bread. **ASK:** Did God keep His promise to Elijah and the widow? Our God keeps His promises!

Show your child a container that might pass as a "jar of flour" or a "jug of oil" (such as a mason jar, a cup with a lid, or a plastic food container). **SAY:** Do you see the bottom of this? If I filled it up, then kept using it, would you see the bottom again? God promised that the widow's jar of flour and jug of oil would never get used up if she obeyed Him, and He kept His promise. It was a miracle!

Practice memorizing the following verse in two different ways—the first as if you are starving, and the second as if God has filled up your tummies with good bread. "My God will meet all your needs" (Philippians 4:19 NIV). **ASK:** How has God met our family's needs today?

Prayer

Thank You, God, for meeting our needs. Help us to trust You for everything, including the food we eat. Thank You for loving us and taking care of us. Amen.

God Proves His Power

Elijah approached the people and said, "How long will you not decide between two choices? If the LORD is the true God, follow Him, but if Baal is the true God, follow him!" **1 KINGS 18:21**

God's people forgot about Him and started praying to a statue. They thought it was God and that it could hear them. God didn't like this, so He sent Elijah to show them that they were wrong. Elijah arranged a contest. Each group was supposed to set up an altar with a bull on it, and whoever sent fire from heaven to burn up the altar was the one true God. The people who prayed to the statue called to it all day, but it couldn't hear them—it couldn't send down fire from heaven because it was a piece of rock. But then Elijah prayed. He asked God to show the people that He is God, so they would start to love God again. And God did something amazing: He sent down a huge fire from heaven—whoosh—that burned up everything on the altar! Then God's people remembered Him and worshiped Him.

Read the paraphrase and/or act out the story together. **ASK:** What does this story show us about God?

Read 1 Kings 18:25-29. **ASK:** Why do you think no one answered these guys? Were they praying to the real God?

Read 1 Kings 18:30-35. **ASK:** Do you think that much water would make it hard for God to make a fire there? What happens when we put water on a fire? Why do you think Elijah wanted them to put so much water on?

Read 1 Kings 18:36-39. **SAY:** Wow, do you think the people were surprised that the fire came down and burned up even the water? I bet they were! God sure knows how to show people that He's God!

SAY: God did this whole contest to have His people remember one thing: "The LORD is God!" (verse 39). The people were so surprised that God had done such an amazing thing that they actually fell down on their faces and worshiped God. Let's try that. Together, lay face down on the ground and say "The LORD is God!" (Kings 18:39).

Prayer

God, You are so amazing! You are the only real and true God, and You listen to us when we call on You. Help us to only pray to You, always. Amen.

God Speaks to Elijah

The LORD said to Elijah, "Go, stand in front of me on the mountain, and I will pass by you." **1 KINGS 19:11**

Elijah was very sad. He felt like he was the only person left who loved God. He went out to a cave on a mountain to complain to God. While he was there, God promised to pass by. A great and powerful wind tore the mountains apart and broke rocks, but God was not in the great wind. After the wind, an earthquake shook the mountain, but God was not in the earthquake. After the earthquake there was a crackling fire, but God was not in the fire. After the fire came a gentle whisper. When Elijah heard it, he pulled his coat over his face and went out of the cave, and God spoke to him in a gentle whisper.

Read the paraphrase then act out the story with lots of dramatic effects! **ASK:** Why do you think God spoke in a whisper?

SAY: Elijah went to the cave because he was sad that everyone was disobeying God. Are there some things that make you sad? Talk to God about them now. At the end, ask God to whisper to your heart. Say, is there anything You want to say to me, God?

SAY: Let's practice listening to very quiet things by whispering secrets to each other. Whisper things like "God loves you" and "Jesus wants to be your friend forever" into your child's ear.

Be very quiet and listen to the sounds around you. What do you hear? **ASK:** Why do you think God decided to talk to Elijah in a whisper instead of in a big loud voice? Do you think God CAN speak in a big loud voice? (HINT: Check out Psalm 29:3-4.)

Read the story straight from the Bible (1 Kings 19:11-13) while your child draws a picture of a cave.

Prayer

God, thank You for making the great and powerful things like winds and fires and for making quiet things like whispers. Help us to hear Your whisper in our hearts. Help our hearts and minds to be quiet enough to hear You. Amen.

God Saves a Widow's Family

The wife of a man from the groups of prophets said to Elisha, "Your servant, my husband, is dead. You know he honored the LORD. But now the man he owes money to is coming to take my two boys as his slaves!" **2 KINGS 4:1**

A friend of Elisha's died, and his wife had no money for her family. Elisha told her to go find every empty jar she could possibly find; she even asked her neighbors for some. Once her house was full of jars, Elisha told her to pour oil from her tiny jar into the big jars. She poured and poured and poured but the tiny jar of oil didn't run out until the last big jar had been filled. It was a miracle! She was able to sell all the jars of oil and have money for her family.

Read the paraphrase and/or act out the story together. **ASK:** Why do you think God saved this family?

Fill a small cup with water. **ASK:** What would happen if I poured this into a big bucket? Would there still be water in this little cup? Would the bucket be full? When Elisha asked the woman to keep pouring oil from her little jug into ALL those jars, do you think she might have been worried it might run out? Isn't it amazing how God helped this family?

Talk about a difficulty that is facing your child right now. **SAY:** How does that make you feel? Where do you go when you feel sad or angry or all alone? The woman in this story went to Elisha, God's friend, because she knew that God would help her, through Elisha. Let's ask God to help us too.

Read the story straight from the Bible 2 Kings 4:1-7, while your child draws a picture of a jar. **SAY:** God helped the woman, but she had to also obey God. If she hadn't gotten the jars, poured in the oil, and sold the oil, the miracle would not have happened. Is there some way that we can also show obedience to God today?

SAY: God used Elisha to help the widow. Sometimes God wants to use us to help others in need as well. Perhaps someone might like a nice card or a treat. What could we make together this weekend to help this person? Decide on something you can do together, then do it!

Prayer

God, thank You so much for meeting the widow's needs. Thanks for promising to meet all of our needs. Help us to bring our needs to You everyday and allow You to meet them in Your own amazing way. Amen.

God Heals Naaman

Naaman was commander of the army of the king of Aram. He was honored by his master, and he had much respect because the LORD used him to give victory to Aram. He was a mighty and brave man, but he had a skin disease. **2 KINGS 5:1**

Naaman was an important man, but he had a very bad disease called leprosy. His servant girl knew about God's friend Elisha, and she told Naaman that Elisha could heal him. So off he went on a trip to find Elisha. When he came to Elisha's house, Elisha sent out a messenger telling him to go wash himself seven times in the Jordan river. Naaman was SO mad because he thought this was a terrible way to get healed. He wanted Elisha to come out and wave his hands over him instead of making him wash in dirty water. But God was waiting to see if Naaman would be humble and follow his instructions. Finally, Naaman did what Elisha said, and God healed him of his leprosy. After that, Naaman decided to become a follower of God.

Read the paraphrase and/or act out the story together. **SAY:** Naaman was actually an enemy of God's people. What does this story show us about God?

Go to a tap and put your hands in the water seven times. **ASK:** How did that feel? Did it feel kind of silly to do the same thing seven times? How did Naaman feel about what Elisha asked him to do? Has your mom or dad ever asked you to do something that you thought was silly but was actually really important?

Read the story straight from the Bible (2 Kings 5:1-3, 9-14) while your child draws a picture of a river. **ASK:** Is it always easy to obey when someone gives us instructions? No way, it sure isn't always easy! What did God want Naaman to do? And what happened when Naaman actually did it?

Practice memorizing Philippians 4:19 (NIV) by saying it in two different ways: first, pretend to be sick like Naaman was. Say together: "My God will meet all your needs." Then pretend to go into the river and dip in seven times. Afterward, recite the verse again. God sure does meet our needs!

SAY: Do we know someone who is sick? They probably don't have leprosy like Naaman, but they still need to know that God loves them. Let's pray for him/her today.

Prayer

Thank You, God, for healing Naaman, and for teaching him to follow You at the same time! Help us to remember that You meet all our needs. Amen

God Gives Jonah a Second Chance

The LORD caused a big fish to swallow Jonah, and Jonah was inside the fish three days and three nights. **JONAH 1:17**

God asked Jonah to do something hard. Jonah didn't want to do it, so he ran away and jumped on a boat. He thought he could hide from God. But God knew where he was and sent a big storm after him. The sailors on the boat thought the storm would kill them, so Jonah said "if you throw me in the water, God will stop the storm." When they tossed him in, God saved Jonah by sending a big fish to gulp him down. After three days inside the fish, Jonah told God that he was sorry for running away. God gave Jonah a second chance to do the hard thing and had the fish spit Jonah out onto a beach so he could go do it.

Read the paraphrase and/or act out the story together. **ASK:** Why do you think God decided to give Jonah another chance to obey?

SAY: Jonah tried to hide from God. Do you think that's a good idea? Let's see if we can think of some place in our house where God couldn't find us. (If you have time, play a game of hide-and-seek with your child and remind him/her that God is always with them!)

Put some water in a sink or a large bowl and encourage your child to blow bubbles in the bowl. **ASK:** How would you feel if you got tossed in the ocean and didn't know how to swim? Do you think Jonah knew the fish was going to swallow him?

Go find the stinkiest garbage can in your house and have your child sniff it. **SAY:** The inside of a fish is not a nice place to be! It might smell a little bit like this garbage can, ew! Let's imagine that we're inside the fish with Jonah. What can we see/smell/taste/touch/hear?

SAY: In the end, Jonah repented and did what God had asked him to do. "Repented" means that he said that he was sorry and that he wouldn't disobey again. Is there something that you need to repent of or someone that you need to say "sorry" to? God gave Jonah a second chance after he repented. He will do that for you too.

Prayer

Thank You, God, for showing Jonah that your way really is the best way! Help us to trust and obey you always. Amen.

God Protects in the Fiery Furnace

Shadrach, Meshach, and Abednego answered the king, saying, "Nebuchadnezzar, we do not need to defend ourselves to you. If you throw us into the blazing furnace, the God we serve is able to save us from the furnace. He will save us from your power, O king." **DANIEL 3:16-17**

The king made a giant statue out of metal and made people worship it, pretending that it was God. Everyone had to bow down before the statue or else they would be thrown into a fire. Most people obeyed and bowed down to the statue, but there were three men who would not. Shadrach, Meshach, and Abednego refused to bow down to the statue because they knew the real God wouldn't like that. The king got SUPER angry, and he told the soldiers to throw the three men into a fiery furnace. It was so hot that even the soldiers who threw them into the fire got burnt. But not Shadrach, Meshach, and Abednego! The king peered into the fire, and he was very surprised to see the men walking around, definitely not dead. He was even more surprised to see four men in the fire, not three. He called them out, and the three men stepped out of the fire. They were not burned at all.

After reading the paraphrase to your kids, act out the story together with them. **ASK:** Why do you think God decided to save them?

Read Daniel 3:25 to find out who the king thought was man #4 in the furnace. **ASK:** Do you think he was right? Who else might it have been? Practice memorizing Matthew 28:20: "I will be with you always."

Read the story directly from the Bible (Daniel 3:13-27) while your child draws a picture of a fire. **ASK:** Were the three men scared to go in the furnace? Why not? (The answer is in verses 16-18.)

Read what the king says about God after seeing the great rescue: "No other god can save his people like this!" (verse 29). **ASK:** Do you know someone who needs rescuing? (perhaps from an illness, a situation, or from being far from God) Pray together. **SAY:** "God, we know that there is no one else who can rescue like you. Please rescue ____________________ from ____________________________."

SAY: Shadrach, Meshach, and Abednego obeyed God's rule about only bowing to him instead of the king's rule about bowing down to the statue. Can you think of a time when you chose to obey God? How do you know what God's rules are?

Prayer

Thank You, God, for saving Shadrach,
Meshach, and Abednego. Thank You for helping
them follow You and then saving them.
Thank You for showing everyone that
You are the God who rescues. Amen.

God Saves Daniel

King Darius gave the order, and Daniel was brought in and thrown into the lions' den. The king said to Daniel, "May the God you serve all the time save you!" **DANIEL 6:16**

Daniel worked for a king. He was very good at his job and the king really liked him. But the king's other helpers were jealous of Daniel. They asked the king to make a rule that people could only pray to the king, instead of to God. Daniel did not think it was a great rule, so he went to his room and prayed to God anyway. The king's helpers tattled on him, and the king had to follow his own rule and throw Daniel into a cave full of hungry lions. Oh no! Everyone thought the lions would gobble Daniel up, but God saved Daniel. In the morning everyone was very surprised that Daniel was still alive. God had shut the mouths of the lions. The king took Daniel out of the cave and was so very happy that God had saved him.

After reading the paraphrase to your kids, act Daniel's story out together. **ASK:** What does this story show us about God?

SAY: Daniel prayed to God even though it was against the rules. Did you know that there are still some places in the world where it's against the rules to pray to God? Let's talk to God right now. We'll thank Him that it's not against the rules to pray in our country, and we'll pray that people in other countries would have courage like Daniel to keep talking to God.

Read the story directly from the Bible (Daniel 6:6-23) while your child draws a picture of a lion.

Pretend to be the hungry lions in a cave. Imagine that some tasty food gets dropped in. **ASK:** What happened to the lions when Daniel got dropped in? (Daniel 6:22) Pretend to be the lions after the angel has shut their mouths. How do you think they acted?

Practice memorizing Matthew 28:20—"I will be with you always"—while roaring like lions, with your mouths closed, and while jumping for joy.

Prayer

Thank You, God, for giving Daniel the courage to pray even when he knew it was against the rules. Thank You for saving him from the lions and for teaching the king that we should only pray to You, not to people. Amen.

God Saves His People through Esther

"You may have been chosen queen for just such a time as this." **ESTHER 4:14**

Most children have only heard small parts of the story of Esther. During this week's devotions we'll go through the whole thing so they can find out how God was with Esther! Each day, have your child either draw that part of the story as you read the paraphrase or role-play it with them. If your kids are older, feel free to read straight from the Bible passages referenced. Otherwise, read from the paraphrase.

ESTHER IS CHOSEN: (Esther 2:1-18) The king needed a new queen. He sent his servants out into all his kingdom and had them bring back a whole bunch of girls so he could meet them. The girls spent a whole year having beauty treatments before they even got to meet the king! One of the girls was named Esther, and she was one of God's special people, called the Jews. Lots of the girls wanted to be queen, but the king chose Esther. He was so excited when he met her that he put the crown on her head and declared her queen. To celebrate, he had a huge party!

ASK: What kind of person do you think makes a good king or queen?

HAMAN HATCHES A PLOT: (Esther 3) There was a really bad guy in the kingdom, and his name was Haman. The king didn't know he was a really bad guy, so he put him in charge of lots of important things. Haman really hated the Jews, so he decided to trick the king into having them all killed. Killed!! What a really bad guy. And his plan worked! He tricked the king into making a law that said all the Jews had to be killed.

ASK: How would you feel if someone tricked you into doing something really bad?

ESTHER GOES TO THE KING: (Esther 4:15-5:3) Esther found out about Haman's plan, and she was so scared, because the new law meant that she and all her family would be killed. Yikes! She decided to talk to the king. This was a scary thing to do, because this king didn't like people talking to him unless he invited them into his throne room. If they walked in without being invited, the king was allowed to throw them in jail, and Queen Esther hadn't been invited. First, she asked God to make her brave. Then she dressed in her fanciest clothes and walked into the throne room. When the king saw Queen Esther standing there, he held out his gold scepter, which meant that she was allowed to come in. The king asked her, "What do you want, Queen Esther? What is your request? I will give it to you, even if it is half the kingdom!"

ASK: What would you ask for if the king told you that you were allowed to ask for anything you wanted?

ESTHER HAS A PARTY: (Esther 5:4-8, 7) When the king asked Esther what she wanted, she invited the king and Haman to a special party. Of course, they were quite excited about this. Then she invited them to another party. At this second party, the king finally asked her what she actually wanted. She told him that a really bad guy was trying to kill her and her people, and that she wanted the king to save her. The king was shocked! Who would want to kill his wonderful queen? Esther pointed at Haman and said, "This wicked Haman is our enemy." The king finally figured out that he had been tricked by the really bad guy. He got rid of Haman and saved the Jews. Hooray!

ASK: How would you feel if someone saved your life?

SAY: Think of some times in Esther's story where she had to be brave. In Matthew 28:20, God says "I will be with you always." How do you think God helped Esther?

Prayer

Thank You, God, for being with
Esther and for giving her courage.
Thank You for making her the queen
so she was able to save the Jews.
You think of everything God! Help us to trust
You even when we're afraid. Amen.

God Sends Nehemiah

The wall of Jerusalem was completed on the twenty-fifth day of the month of Elul. It took fifty-two days to rebuild. When all our enemies heard about it and all the nations around us saw it, they were shamed. They then understood that the work had been done with the help of our God. **NEHEMIAH 6:15-16**

The people of God lived in Jerusalem, but its walls were old and broken down. Their enemies hadn't allowed them to rebuild their walls because they didn't want the people in Jerusalem to be strong. After many years, God told Nehemiah to rebuild the wall. All the people of Jerusalem helped out, building it up stone by stone so it could protect them again. Their enemies tried to stop them, but Nehemiah kept praying to God for help. To keep the wall builders safe, half the people worked on the wall and the other half protected the builders. Even the men carrying stones kept their swords at their side. With God's help, they finished building the wall around the whole city in just 52 days!

After reading the paraphrase to your kids, act out Nehemiah's story together. **ASK:** Why do you think God wanted Nehemiah to rebuild the walls around Jerusalem?

Ask your child to sneak very quietly around the room while you read Nehemiah 2:11-18. **SAY:** Nehemiah knew God's enemies wouldn't want him to rebuild the wall, so he had to inspect it in secret, at night. Why would God's enemies be mad about this?

SAY: When Nehemiah told everyone that God wanted them to rebuild the wall, all God's people joined in as a big team. Let's imagine we're building a wall together. Use imaginary rocks or actual toy blocks. **SAY:** We might not be rebuilding walls, but we're still part of God's team. What do we do as part of God's team?

Read Nehemiah 4:12-21 while your child draws a picture of the passage. After, **ASK:** Tell me about your drawing. Why did you draw that part? What's your favorite part of what we read today?

Read Nehemiah 4:15-16. **ASK:** How long did it take to build a wall around the whole city? How did God help them? What do you need God to help you with right now?

Prayer

Thank You, God, for helping Nehemiah and his team build the wall around Jerusalem. It was a hard job, and they were surrounded by enemies, but You helped and kept them safe. Help us to trust You when we have hard jobs too. Amen.

God Gives Clues about Jesus

But He was wounded for the wrong we did; He was crushed for the evil we did. The punishment, which made us well, was given to Him, and we are healed because of His wounds. ISAIAH 53:5

Do you remember that big word we learned a long time ago: SIN? Sin is when we choose to disobey God. Adam and Eve sinned, and so has every other person. Sin is sad because it pulls us away from God. But guess what? God made a way to fix our sin so we can be with Him again. He sent Jesus, which is what the second part of the Bible is all about. But Jesus didn't just come out of nowhere. The first part of the Bible is full of clues about what Jesus would do and how He would save us. This week we're going to look at some of these clues, which God gave hundreds of years before Jesus was even born!

Read Micah 5:2. **ASK:** Where does it say the ruler would be born? And do you know where Jesus was born? In Bethlehem! Let's find Bethlehem on a map. Pull up Bethlehem on an online map and see how far away it is from you.

Read Isaiah 35:5-6. **ASK:** What are the things God promised would happen when Jesus came? Can you tell me a story of when Jesus did one of those things?

Read Zechariah 9:9 and act it out. **SAY:** God told Zechariah that Jesus was going to be a gentle king who rode a donkey instead of a war horse. If your child isn't familiar with Palm Sunday, feel free to tell the story now.

Read Isaiah 53:5. **SAY:** God told Isaiah that Jesus would die and that the punishment for our sin would go on Him. Imagine you disobeyed me and instead of you going in time-out, I put myself in time-out. That would be weird because I didn't do anything bad. But that's what Jesus did for us. He didn't do anything bad but He took our punishment so we could be with God.

Read 2 Samuel 7:12-13. **SAY:** God told King David that one day someone from his family would have a kingdom that lasts forever. That's Jesus! Let's bow down to our King Jesus. Bow low. This would be a great time to pray.

Prayer

Thank You, God, for sending so many clues about what Jesus would be like. Thank You for saving us. Help us to know what that means. Amen.

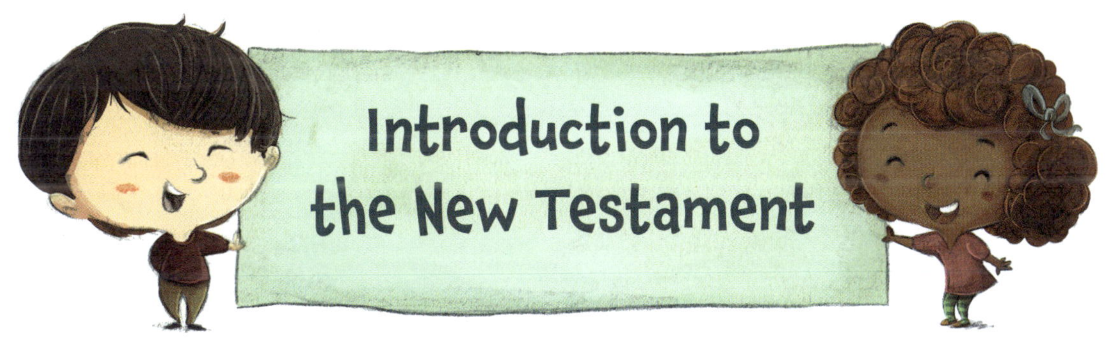

The second part of the Bible is called the New Testament. It's the part of the Bible that was written after Jesus was born.

The first part of the New Testament tells us all about how God sent His only Son, Jesus. Jesus showed God's love to everyone He met, and eventually, He showed His love to the whole world by dying on the cross for us. The best part is, Jesus didn't stay dead! After He came back to life, He went back to heaven to prepare a place for you and me, and He sent the Holy Spirit to comfort, guide, teach, and intercede on behalf of His followers.

The rest of the New Testament is about the Holy Spirit doing amazing things through Jesus' followers, and how you and I can live with Jesus' Spirit inside us too.

God Sends an Angel to Mary

The angel said to Mary, "The Holy Spirit will come upon you, and the power of the Most High will cover you. For this reason the baby will be holy and will be called the Son of God." **LUKE 1:35**

One day, a lady named Mary was doing work at home, maybe sweeping the floor or washing clothes. Suddenly, something super bright was standing right in front of her! She freaked out a bit, but the shiny thing turned out to be an angel from God. He told her God had chosen her to do something very special. He said God wanted Mary to have a baby, even though she wasn't married yet. She was pretty confused, but God really wanted her to have this baby. See, this baby wasn't just any old baby. It was God's own Son. This baby was going to be the Savior! God had chosen Mary for a very special job—she would get to be the mom of God's Son, and she would call Him Jesus.

Read the paraphrase or read this portion of the Christmas story from a picture Bible. **ASK:** What does this story show us about God?

Mary would have been very excited about the birth of her Son, just as we get excited to celebrate His birthday. With your child, put together a paper chain with one link for each day before Christmas. Remember to take off one link each day! **ASK:** Are you excited about Christmas? Why?

ACT out the story together, with one person being Mary and one as the angel. Mary could be doing chores when the angel surprises her with some amazing news. Put your emotions into it and really imagine how you might feel if an angel visited you.

Have your child draw a picture of an angel while you read Luke 1:26-33, 38. **ASK:** How do you think Mary felt when the angel appeared?

Mary reacted to this good news by writing a worship song. Together with your child, write a song or poem of worship to God.

Prayer

God, thank You for choosing Mary, an ordinary person, to be the mommy of Your Son. Thank You for loving the world so much that You sent Your Son to live with us. Help us to remember that You are the reason we have Christmas! Amen.

Jesus Is Born

While they were in Bethlehem, the time came for Mary to have the baby, and she gave birth to her first son. Because there were no rooms left in the inn, she wrapped the baby with pieces of cloth and laid Him in a feeding trough. LUKE 2:6-7

Just before Mary had her baby, the king decided he wanted everyone in the country to be counted and pay taxes, but they had to be in their hometown. So Mary and Joseph left their town and went to Bethlehem, which is where Joseph's family was from. While they were there, Mary had her baby. Sadly, since there were so many people in Bethlehem, there was no room in anyone's house for them to sleep in. But someone did let them stay with the animals. Only the newborn Savior ended up with a bed that night, and it was a manger—the place where people kept the food for their animals! They named Him Jesus, just as the angel had said.

Pretend that you are Mary and Joseph and take a long walk through your home. When you reach your child's bedroom, shut the door and say, "There's no room here! I guess we'll have to rest in the hallway." **ASK:** What do you think it was like for Mary to go on a long trip with a baby in her tummy? How does it feel to be told that there's no room for you?

Find a nativity scene and use it to reenact the story. **ASK:** What do you like the best about the story?

Have your child draw a picture of a baby while you read Luke 2:1-7. **ASK:** Why do you think Mary wrapped Jesus up? How do we take care of babies in our country?

Pretend to be farm animals together. Then **ASK:** Where do women normally have babies? Do you think Mary was surprised to have her baby where the animals lived? How do you think it smelled? Was it warm or cold? Do you think Mary was scared? Why or why not? Sing "Away in a Manger" together.

Find a baby doll or a stuffed animal and a box or laundry basket. Put the doll in the basket, pretending that it is baby Jesus in the manger. Gather around the box then pray: Thank You so much, Jesus, for coming, and for being born with the animals instead of in a castle. Thank You for loving us so much that You would come down from heaven to live with us. We love You so much Jesus.

Prayer

Thank You, God, for protecting Mary and Joseph on their long trip. And we most especially thank You for the gift of Your Son, Jesus. Amen.

Angels Speak to Shepherds

When the angels left them and went back to heaven, the shepherds said to each other, "Let's go to Bethlehem. Let's see this thing that has happened which the Lord has told us about." **LUKE 2:15**

One dark and quiet night, shepherds cared for their sheep in a field. Suddenly, a bright light blasted in their faces and an angel spoke to them! The angel told them of an extra special baby who had just been born, and that they should go visit Him. The baby's name was Jesus. Then even more angels joined the first one and they sang praises to God. After they left, the sky grew dark, and the field became quiet again. The shepherds were so excited that they jumped up and ran to Bethlehem to see baby Jesus. After they saw Him, they told everyone they knew that Jesus had been born!

Pretend you are shepherds taking care of sheep. **ASK:** What do shepherds do for their sheep? What do they do when the sheep are hungry? Thirsty? Tired? Jesus says that He is like our shepherd, and He takes care of us like shepherds take care of their sheep.

Turn off the lights in your room and have your child pretend to be sleeping. Suddenly, turn on the lights or a bright flashlight and tell your child what the angel said. **ASK:** Did I surprise you? How do you think the shepherds felt when the angel showed up? Sing

"Angels We Have Heard on High" or another angel Christmas carol with your child.

After the shepherds heard about Jesus' birth, they had to go find Him. Hide a small doll or toy somewhere and have your child go find "baby Jesus." **ASK:** How do you think the shepherds felt when they found the baby? How would you feel if you got to see the real baby Jesus?

Draw the shape of a shepherd's staff (with a crook). Show your child the similarity between the candy cane shape and the shepherd's staff. **SAY:** The man who invented the candy cane made it in the shape of a shepherd's staff to remind us that shepherds visited the baby Jesus at His birth! If we look at the candy cane upside down, what letter does it look like? A *J*! And who's name starts with *J*? Jesus!

Read this part of the Christmas story in a children's Bible. **ASK:** I wonder why God showed these shepherds how to find Jesus? What does this story show us about God?

Prayer

Thank You, God, for telling Your great news to ordinary people. Thank You for loving the world so much that You sent Your Son. Help us to remember You, the best present of all this Christmas. Amen.

God Leads Wise Men to Jesus

They came to the house where the child was and saw Him with His mother, Mary, and they bowed down and worshiped Him. **MATTHEW 2:11**

When Jesus was born, people noticed a new, beautiful star shining brightly in the sky. Some wise men from far away saw the star and knew it meant a new King had been born. They packed up some camping supplies and went on the long journey to find the baby King. They followed the star right to the place where baby Jesus was living. When they saw Him, they bowed down and worshiped Him and gave Him wonderful gifts.

Pretend to be the wise men and go on a little journey through your house, looking for baby Jesus. **ASK:** How do you think the wise men felt on their long trip? What did they think when they finally found the baby they were looking for? Do you think they were surprised that the baby King wasn't living in a castle?

SAY: Do you remember what the wise men followed to find the baby Jesus? Let's sing "Twinkle, Twinkle, Little Star" together to remind us about the amazing sign God put in the sky when Jesus was born!

Have your child draw a picture of a star while you read Matthew 2:1-11. **ASK:** Have you ever been on a long journey? What would you bring with you if you were going to meet a newborn baby?

Read today's story in a children's Bible. **ASK:** I wonder why God showed these men how to find Jesus? What does this story show us about God?

SAY: The wise men brought baby Jesus some interesting gifts—gold, frankincense, and myrrh. Frankincense and myrrh are types of rock that people used as perfume. What kind of gift would you bring the baby Jesus?

Option For Families With Multiple Children:
Have your child choose one of their special toys that they can gift to another child in the family. **ASK:** Why do we give gifts at Christmas? What makes a good gift?

Prayer

God, You are so amazing. Only You can put a star in the sky for people from another country to follow. Thank You for showing these wise men the baby Jesus. Thank You that You care about and love everyone. Amen.

Jesus Obeys His Father

After the feast days were over, they started home. The boy Jesus stayed behind in Jerusalem, but His parents did not know it. LUKE 2:43

When Jesus was only twelve years old, His family traveled a long way to Jerusalem for a big party called the Passover. But when they left, Jesus stayed behind! His parents searched everywhere for three whole days. They were worried they would never find Him. Finally, they looked in the temple, and there He was! He was teaching the adults about God. His parents were kind of angry with Him, but He told them that He was being obedient to His Father in heaven. God wanted Jesus to teach others about Him, and Jesus was obeying.

While you read Luke 2:41-50, have your child draw a squiggly line around the paper showing all the places that Mary and Joseph looked for Jesus. **SAY:** How do you think Jesus' parents felt when they lost Him? How do you think they felt when they found Him?

Act out the story with your child or have some dolls or stuffed animals act it out for you. See how much your child can tell you from memory. **ASK:** What is your favorite part of this story? Why?

ASK: Have you ever been lost somewhere, and you didn't know where your parents were? (If not, help your child imagine a situation in which they are lost in a grocery store or in the middle of a big crowd.) How did you feel? Do you think Jesus felt scared or not?

ASK: When Jesus' parents found Him, what was Jesus doing? When Jesus talked about God with the people in the temple, He was doing what God wanted Him to do. When we obey God like Jesus did, we show love to Him. How do you show love to God?

Read Luke 2:52. **SAY:** Jesus was able to grow in favor with God and people because He knew God's Word. Let's practice memorizing this verse together: "Loving God means obeying his commands" (1 John 5:3).

Prayer

Dear Jesus, You are so amazing. Thank You for showing us how to love God—by telling everyone about Your Word and by obeying You. Help us to love You and obey You. Amen.

Jesus Loves Children

When Jesus saw this, He was upset and said to them, "Let the little children come to Me. Don't stop them, because the kingdom of God belongs to people who are like these children. MARK 10:14

One day Jesus was standing around with a big crowd of people around Him. Some mamas and papas brought their children to Jesus, hoping He would pray for them. Jesus' friends thought He was WAY too important to talk to children, so they told the kids to go away! But Jesus said "Hey guys, I LOVE kids! Let them come see Me!" Then He put His hands on their heads and blessed the children.

Act out the story using yourselves, stuffies, or dolls. **ASK:** Why do you think the kids wanted to see Jesus? If you had been there, would you have waited quietly in line to see Jesus or would you have jumped all over Him and given Him a hug? What would you have said to Him?

ASK: How old are you? Do you think Jesus loves you? How about after your next birthday, how old will you be then? Will Jesus still love you? How about the birthday after that? Will Jesus love me when I've had my next birthday? Does God love a baby who hasn't had any birthdays at all? God loves us no matter how many birthdays we've had!

Read Mark 10:13-16 out loud. **ASK:** Who is the king in the Kingdom of God? What do you think the Kingdom of God is like? (NOTE for parents: the Kingdom of God refers to God's Kingdom here on earth, not just heaven. Help your child imagine what would happen if love, joy, peace, patience, kindness, goodness, faithfulness, gentleness, and self-control were seen everywhere. What would this look like?) **ASK:** Would you like to be part of the Kingdom of God?

Using a piece of paper, some scissors, and tape, make a crown with/for your child. Read Mark 10:14. **ASK:** Did you know that you are a prince/princess in the Kingdom of God? How does that make you feel?

SAY: Just like Jesus blessed the children, I want to bless you too. Take your child in your arms, put your hands on them, and bless them, saying, "May the Lord bless you and keep you. May the Lord show you His kindness and have mercy on you. May the Lord watch over you and give you peace" (Numbers 6:24-26). If you haven't already gotten into the habit of blessing your child, try doing this every night. You'll be surprised at how much your child will love being blessed and how much you are blessed in return.

Prayer

Thank You, Jesus, for loving me! I love You too. Amen.

Jesus Cares for Us

"So I tell you, don't worry about the food or drink you need to live, or about the clothes you need for your body. Life is more than food, and the body is more than clothes." **MATTHEW 6:25**

Jesus liked to tell people how much God loved them. One time He talked about how God takes care of the birds and flowers. Birds don't have to go grocery shopping or go to a restaurant to buy food, because God takes care of them and helps them find food in nature. And flowers don't have to go to the store to buy warm clothes in winter or pretty clothes for summer. God takes care of them and makes them beautiful. Just like God takes care of the birds and flowers, He wants us to know that He will care for us too.

Pretend to be birds! Fly around pecking seeds off the floor. Finish up by sitting down on a "branch" and tuck your head under your "wings." **ASK:** How does God take care of the birds? How does God take care of you and me?

Read the verses from the Matthew 6:25-34 while your child draws a picture of a flower or a bird. **ASK:** What do you like most about this story that Jesus told?

Have your child pretend to be a flower. Show them how to start as a tiny seed and then slowly grow as you give them water and sunshine. **ASK:** Do you think this flower worries about how much water and sunshine it's going to get? Just like God provides these flowers with what they need to grow, God will provide you with what you need to grow. What DO you need to grow?

If you have access to flowers outside, clip one and bring it to devotions with you. If not, just pretend to have one or look up some pictures. Talk about what color it is, how pretty it looks, and how God made it special and takes care of it.

Practice the following verse while acting like a bird or flower. "My God will meet all your needs" (Philippians 4:19 NIV).

Prayer

Thank You, God, for taking care of the birds and flowers, and for taking care of us. Help us to trust You with our needs. Amen.

God's Most Important Rules

One Pharisee, who was an expert on the law of Moses, asked Jesus this question to test Him: "Teacher, which command in the law is the most important?" **MATTHEW 22:35-36**

Some of the leaders of Israel got together and asked Jesus a question. They asked, "which is the most important rule in the Bible?" Jesus answered them: "'Love the Lord your God with all your heart, all your soul, and all your mind.' This is the first and most important command. And the second command is like the first: 'Love your neighbor as you love yourself'" (Matthew 22:37-39).

Read Matthew 22:34-39 right out of the Bible. **SAY:** Do you remember what the two most important rules are that Jesus gave? Love God and love other people. Help your child draw a picture of a heart to remind yourselves that God's most important rules are about love.

SAY: The first and most important rule is to love God. Let's make a valentine card for God! Help your child write "I love You, God" or something similar from their heart. Post it up in their room to remind them about how they love God!

Reenact the story with your child, with you asking the questions posed by the leaders and with your child pretending to be Jesus. See how much of Jesus' answer your child can remember! Prompt as much as necessary. **SAY:** If you got to make up any rule for the whole world, what would your rule be? What do you think the leaders thought of Jesus' rule?

SAY: The second rule that Jesus talks about is to love your neighbor. Who is your neighbor? (Most preschoolers will take this literally to mean "person who lives next door." Go with that for now, as there will be opportunities to teach the more abstract meaning of the word in other devotions.) What can we do to love our neighbor today? (You could make a card for your neighbor or plan to do something nice the next day.)

SAY: How can we show love to God today? (Together, think of something your child can do that would be God-honoring. Perhaps it would be singing "Jesus Loves Me" or practicing the memory verse. Let your child come up with the answer!)

Prayer

Dear God, we love You so much. Please help us to love You and to love our neighbors. Amen.

Jesus Calls His Disciples

Jesus chose twelve and called them apostles. **MARK 3:14**

After Jesus started teaching people about the Kingdom of God, He chose twelve men to stay with Him to watch Him teach, heal, pray, and do miracles. This week we are going to learn the stories of how those men came to follow Him!

With your child (or using stuffed animals/dolls), act out the story of Jesus calling the fishermen found in Mark 1:16-20. **ASK:** What does a fisherman do? What kind of jobs do the people in our family do? Do you think Jesus wants us to follow Him too, even though we're not fishermen? Yes, He does!

With your child (or using stuffed animals/dolls), act out the story of Jesus calling Levi found in Luke 5:27-29. **SAY:** Tax collectors were people that nobody liked because they usually took extra money from people. Why do you think Jesus wanted to be friends with a tax collector? How can we show God's love to people that aren't very likable?

Read the following Scripture as dramatically as possible: John 1:43-50. **SAY:** Jesus showed Nathaniel a miracle—He knew what Nathaniel was doing even though He was far away. Can you do that? Do you think you would have followed Jesus if He told you something like that? Why or why not?

Help your child draw a picture of Jesus and His twelve friends. **ASK:** Why do you think Jesus wanted twelve friends? Who do you think Jesus wants to be His friend today? (you, me, our family, others)

In Matthew 28:20 Jesus says, "I will be with you always." It's a promise Jesus made to His first disciples, and it's a promise He makes to us too, because He loves us. Help your child memorize the verse and remind them of Jesus' great love for His first friends and for us!

Prayer

Dear Jesus, thank You for choosing twelve special friends when You were here on earth, and thank You for choosing me to be Your friend forever too! Help me to show others what it means to be Your friend forever. Amen.

Jesus Teaches How to Pray

"So when you pray, you should pray like this..." **MATTHEW 6:9**

Jesus taught His followers about prayer. He said to pray to God without worrying about what other people think and to pray what is really important to us, not pretend words that don't mean anything. Then He gave an example of a prayer. We will go through that prayer this week.

Read Matthew 6:9-10 paraphrased: "You are our Great Big God. Please be in charge of the world just like You're already in charge of heaven." **SAY:** When we tell God that He is our Great Big God, that is a way of saying "I praise You." **ASK:** What are some other things that you could say to God? What do you like best about God? What's really cool about Him? (Draw or write these things onto a piece of paper and write "I Praise You" at the top.)

Read Matthew 6:11 paraphrased: "Please give us what we need every day." **SAY:** God tells us that He wants to answer our prayers. What are some things that you could ask God to help you with today? (Draw or write these things onto a piece of paper and write "Help Me" at the top.)

Read Matthew 6:12-13 paraphrased: "Please forgive us for the bad things we've done and help us forgive people who have done bad things to us. Help us to be good." **SAY:** When we do something bad, something that hurts someone else, we have to apologize to them. But we also need to apologize to God because when we do bad things, it hurts God's heart. What is something that you can apologize to God for? (Draw or write these things onto a piece of paper and write "I'm Sorry" at the top.)

SAY: Colossians 3:15 says "be thankful." God tells us a lot of times in the Bible that we need to thank Him for what He's given us and done for us. What is something that you enjoyed today that you can thank God for? (Draw or write these things onto a piece of paper and write "Thank You" at the top.)

Today, try to do all 4 sections of the prayer: I Praise You, Help Me, I'm Sorry, and Thank You. Continue to use this routine whenever you pray with your child to help them understand the different aspects of prayer.

Jesus Finds the Fish

When Jesus had finished speaking, He said to Simon, "Take the boat into deep water, and put your nets in the water to catch some fish." LUKE 5:4

One day Jesus was sitting in a boat near the shore, teaching people. When He was done, He asked Peter to move the boat and to put his fishing nets in the water. Peter wasn't sure about this. He had already fished all night long and not found a single fish. He really needed to catch fish because fishing was his job, and he needed to sell some fish to feed his family. So he did as Jesus asked, and suddenly there were so many fish that the nets began to break! When they pulled the fish into the boat, it started to sink because there were so many fish flopping around. Wow!

Review the story then act it out with stuffed animals or yourselves as characters. **ASK:** What does this story show us about Jesus?

Gather up a small blanket and several stuffed animals. Together with your child, hold the edges of the blanket so it looks like you are holding a fish net. At the beginning, the animals should be sitting on the floor. **SAY:** Jesus' friends didn't know what was going to happen when they obeyed Jesus. But they did it anyway and they learned that Jesus can do anything! Let's think of amazing things God does, and each time we'll throw a "fish" into our "net" to remind us how amazing He is.

Sit on the edge of a bed or chair and pretend to fish with a fishing pole together. **SAY:** Let's pretend that we are fishing with Jesus. What would you like to say to Jesus while we're sitting here with Him? What would Jesus want to say to you?

Read this story directly from the Bible (Luke 5:1-11) or from a children's Bible while your child draws a picture of a fish.

SAY: When Peter saw Jesus' miracle, he realized how many bad things he had done and knelt in front of Jesus. Jesus forgave him and told him that they were going to work together from now on. Let's kneel down in front of Jesus right now and ask forgiveness for the bad things that we have done.

Prayer

Thank You, Jesus, for showing us Your incredible power by filling up those nets with fish! Help us to trust You and to know that we can ask You for help with anything in our lives. Amen.

Jesus Feeds the People

Jesus took the five loaves and two fish and, looking up to heaven, He thanked God for the food. He divided the bread and gave it to His followers for them to give to the people. Then He divided the two fish among them all. **MARK 6:41**

One day Jesus was with His friends, and many other people followed them and wanted to talk to Jesus. Jesus loved them so He started teaching everyone. But it was getting late, and the people were hungry. Jesus' friends thought it would be best to send the people home, but Jesus said to them "YOU give them something to eat." His friends freaked out and went to find whatever food anyone would share. All they could find was five loaves of bread and two fish. Jesus told everyone to sit down, and then He prayed for the food. When they started passing it out, there kept being more and more food until over 5000 people had eaten!

Review the story then act it out with stuffed animals or yourselves as characters. **ASK:** What does this story show us about Jesus?

ASK: If you were really hungry, what would you like to eat? Would you eat bread and fish if you were SUPER hungry? Who gives us the food that we eat? God does! He helps us make money so that we can buy food from the grocery store, and He helps the farmers grow the food that we buy from the store. Let's thank God for feeding us!

Count to the number five together, then again to the number two. **SAY:** That was how many loaves and fish the friends had to share. And how many people were there to feed? 5000!! That's a lot of people. Could you share five loaves and two fish with that many people? No way! Only Jesus can do that because He can do anything. Let's thank Jesus for being so amazing.

Read this story directly from the Bible (Mark 6:30-44) or from a children's Bible while your child draws a picture of the bread and fish.

SAY: The Bible says that Jesus had "compassion" on the people, and that's why He taught them and fed them. Do you know what compassion is? (Compassion is love for others that leads to helping them.) Who is someone that we can have compassion for? How can we help that person?

Prayer

Thank You, Jesus, for being so loving and amazing that You would take a tiny little lunch and use it to feed so many people! Thank You for feeding us too. Amen.

Jesus Walks on Water

Between three and six o'clock in the morning, Jesus came to them, walking on the water, and He wanted to walk past the boat. **MARK 6:48**

After Jesus fed the 5000 people, He sent His disciples in a boat across the lake while He went up on a hill to pray. While the disciples were rowing the boat across the lake, a big wind started to blow. As the wind blew stronger, the waves grew bigger, and it was very hard for them to row. In the middle of the night, Jesus started walking to them, and He walked right on top of the water in the middle of the windy waves! They were really scared, but Jesus said to them, "It's Me! Don't be afraid." And when He got into the boat, the wind stopped right away. Jesus' friends were completely amazed!

Review the story then act it out with stuffed animals or yourselves as characters. **ASK:** What does this story show us about Jesus?

Put a little water in your bathtub or sink. **ASK:** If we stepped in this, would we sink or float? Do you think we can walk on the water? No way! Isn't Jesus amazing?

Trace your child's foot on a piece of paper (preferably blue). Draw waves underneath it. **ASK:** What does this have to do with the story we've been learning this week? Put the picture up on a wall to remind you of how powerful Jesus is!

Read the story from the Bible (Mark 6:45-51) or from a children's Bible while your child draws a picture of wind and waves.

ASK: Do you know what I think about when I think about Jesus walking on the water? I know that if He can walk on the water then He can do anything. So when we need help we can ask Jesus to help us. Can you think of anything that you (or someone else) need(s) help with? Pray together, asking Jesus to help with the fear or struggle.

Prayer

Jesus, You are so amazing! I don't know anyone else who can walk on water. Thank You for showing us Your incredible power and for helping us when we are afraid. Amen.

Jesus Calms a Storm

Jesus answered, "Why are you afraid? You don't have enough faith." Then Jesus got up and gave a command to the wind and the waves, and it became completely calm. MATTHEW 8:26

Jesus got into a boat with His friends and settled down to take a nap. Suddenly, a crazy storm blew up and Jesus' friends were really scared! Strangely enough, Jesus kept snoozing right through the storm. The disciples woke Him up and said "Save us! We're going to drown!" Jesus stood up and told the wind and waves to be quiet, and they did! Everything became completely calm. Jesus' friends were totally amazed.

Review the story then act it out with stuffed animals or yourselves as characters. **ASK:** What does this story show us about Jesus?

ASK: What does the Bible say that Jesus was doing in the back of the boat? Can you sleep in a storm? Let's pretend that I'm sleeping, and you can try to wake me up by telling me that something big is going to happen.

Pretend to be on a boat and make a storm by slapping your knees and making wind sounds. Together, make the noise and movement stop and start on command. **ASK:** Can you believe that Jesus could just say one word and the storm would stop? I mean, imagine waves crashing, wind blowing, thunder and lightning booming, and rain pouring. Then all of a sudden Jesus tells the storm to stop, and it does! Jesus had power over a storm!

Read this story directly from the Bible [Matthew 8:23-27] or from a children's Bible while your child draws a picture of a storm.

SAY: When you're scared, remember that Jesus loves you, He wants to help you, and He is VERY, VERY strong. Remember, in our story we found out that Jesus was stronger than a HUGE storm. So whenever we are afraid, we can think about how much Jesus loves us, how strong He is, and how He takes care of us, and we can pray and ask Him to help us. What scary thing would you like to pray about right now?

Prayer

Thank You, Jesus, that You take care of us. Even when it sometimes feels like You're asleep on the job, help us to see how You are working in our lives. Amen.

Jesus' Story of a Neighbor

But the man, wanting to show the importance of his question, said to Jesus, "And who is my neighbor?" LUKE 10:29

A man asked Jesus about the most important rules, and Jesus said, "Love God and love others." The man wondered who he was supposed to love, and Jesus told him a story about a man.

The man was walking from one town to another when some robbers beat him up and stole everything from him. He was very badly hurt. The important people wouldn't stop to help him, and the holy people wouldn't stop to help him. But someone that he didn't like stopped to help him! The man, called a Samaritan, put bandages on him and cared for him.

Jesus used this story to teach us who we are supposed to love—everyone, no matter who they are.

Read Luke 10:30-35 while your child draws a picture of a bandage. **ASK:** How does it make you feel when two people walk right by the hurt man and don't help him? Why? How do you think the man felt when he had to wait a long time to get help? **ASK:** What does this story show us about God? How do you think God wants us to help others this week?

Read Luke 10:27-29 and 36-37. **ASK:** Who is your neighbor? God tells us that loving our neighbor doesn't just mean loving the people who live next door: it means loving everyone. Let's think of three people that you can show love to today.

Act out the story with your child, with one of you pretending to be the robbed man and the other(s) being the other characters in the story. **ASK:** What do you think God likes best about this story? What does this story teach us about God?

Read Luke 10:31-32. **ASK:** Why do you think those two men ignored the guy who was hurt? Do we sometimes ignore others when they are hurt? Why? Together, pray that God would help you see those who need help and give you courage to help them.

Act out some scenarios of someone needing help and help your child to think of a way they could help the person.

—you fell off a bike and hurt yourself

—you are sad

—you are in a bad mood

—you are very hungry and don't have any food

Prayer

***Thank You, God, for loving everyone,
not just the people who love You back.
Help us to be like You and
treat others with love. Amen.***

Jesus' Story of a Lost Sheep

"Suppose one of you has a hundred sheep but loses one of them. Then he will leave the other ninety-nine sheep in the open field and go out and look for the lost sheep until he finds it." LUKE 15:4

Jesus told a lot of stories to the people who came to see Him so they could understand God better. One of the stories is about a shepherd who had one hundred sheep. That's a lot of sheep! But one day, one of the sheep went missing. Did the shepherd say, "Oh well, I still have lots of sheep"? No way! He went looking high and low for his little lost sheep. And when he found it, he carried it home on his shoulders. He was so excited that he told all his friends and neighbors about his sheep being found. That's how God feels about us.

Read the paraphrase, and then reenact the story together, using stuffed animals as your "flock." **ASK:** Why do you think the shepherd went to go find his sheep?

Talk about a time when your child was lost or lost something that was important to them. **ASK:** How did you feel when you (or the object) were lost? Was it scary? How did you get found (or find your object)? It says right here in the Bible that if we are lost, God will look for us and keep looking for us until He finds us. The Bible tells us that we are so special to God.

Read the story directly from the Bible (Luke 15:3-7) or a picture Bible while your child draws a picture of a sheep.

Hide a stuffed animal then have your child go and look for it. Celebrate when it is found! Remind your child of the following truth: "He will not leave you or forget you" (Deuteronomy 31:8).

SAY: Let's think about all the places you could hide from me. Is there anywhere in this house that you could hide where I wouldn't be able to find you? No, I would eventually find you wherever you were! In the same way, God always wants to be with you, and He will go searching for you if you try to hide from Him! How does that make you feel?

Prayer

***God, thank You for loving me so very much.
Thank You that I am special to You and that You love me just as much as the shepherd in the story loved his sheep. Amen.***

Jesus' Story of a Lost Son

The younger son said to his father, "Give me my share of the property." So the father divided the property between his two sons. **LUKE 15:12**

Jesus told a lot of stories to the people who came to see Him, so they could understand God better. One of the stories Jesus told is about a boy who decided he didn't want to live with his family anymore, so he asked for a bunch of money from his dad and ran away from home. He was happy with his life for a while, but eventually his money ran out. The people he thought were his friends left him and he didn't know what to do. He took a job feeding pigs and was so hungry he wished he could eat pig food. Yuck. This part of the story shows us that sometimes we don't like being with God, and we run away. But running away from God is never a good idea!

Read the paraphrase, and then act the story together. **ASK:** Why do you think the son wanted to leave his family?

Talk about a time when you disobeyed someone (like God or a parent), and then encourage your child to think of a time when he/she disobeyed. Remind him/her that God loves us even when we do wrong things.

ASK: Do you think the boy's daddy was mad at him when he left? Do you think he said "Go away, I never want to see you again." No? How do you think the daddy felt when the boy left? That's how God feels when we disobey Him! But He still loves us.

Read the story directly from the Bible (Luke 15:11-19) or from a children's Bible while your child draws a picture of the sad, hungry boy. (Be sure to stop reading before the son goes home—that's for another week!)

SAY: Let's pretend that you are a pig and I am the lost boy who has to feed you. (Really ham it up here as you pretend to be the lost boy.) Oh, I'm SO hungry. I wish I could eat a bit of that pig food. It looks so gross but just a little bit, maybe? What's that? I'm not allowed to eat the pig food even? Oh no, but I'm SO hungry! **ASK:** Oh pig, what do you think I should do?

Prayer

Thank You, God, for loving me even when I make mistakes and do wrong things. Amen.

Jesus' Story of a Found Son

While the son was still a long way off, his father saw him and felt sorry for his son. LUKE 15:20

Jesus told a lot of stories to the people who came to see Him, so they could understand God better. Remember that story about the boy who ran away from home? His life became awful, so he decided to go home and apologize to his dad. He thought his dad would be really mad at him. But when he was still a long way away, his daddy saw him coming. He ran to his son and threw his arms around him! He gave him a big kiss, gave him some new clothes and even a special ring. The dad was so excited his son had returned home that he threw a giant party to show the world how happy he was.

Read the paraphrase, and then reenact the story of the lost son together. **ASK:** Why do you think the son was scared to come home? Why wasn't the daddy angry?

Have your child stand on the other side of the room and pretend to be hungry. Then have them run to you while you open your arms and say, "welcome home!" Remind them that God will always love us, no matter what.

Remind your child of the following truth: "He will not leave you or forget you" (Deuteronomy 31:8). **ASK:** How does the dad in this story act like God?

Read the story directly from the Bible (Luke 15:20-24) or from a children's Bible while your child draws a picture of their favorite part of a party (like some balloons or a cake).

ASK: What did the daddy in this story do to show his son that he loved him? (party) What does God do to show you that He loves you?

Prayer

Thank You, God, for loving me SO much. Help us to remember Your great love when we do wrong things and to remember to say that we are sorry for the wrong things we've done. Amen.

Jesus' Story about a Big Party

Jesus said to him, "A man gave a big banquet and invited many people. When it was time to eat, the man sent his servant to tell the guests, 'Come. Everything is ready.'" **LUKE 14:16-17**

Jesus told a lot of stories to the people who came to see Him, so they could understand God better. One of Jesus' stories was about a man who was going to have a great big party. He invited all his friends, but then they all decided that they didn't want to come. The man got really mad because he had set up this super amazing party and none of his friends wanted to come! He decided that he still wanted to have his great party, so he had his servant go and invite all the poor people, the sick people, the blind people, and the people who couldn't walk. After they came, there was still more room, so the man told his servant to bring more and more people until the party was super full.

Read the paraphrase, and then act out the story together. **ASK:** What would you do if someone invited you to a big party? What does this story teach us about God?

ASK: If you wanted to show your friends that you loved them, what would you do for them? Try to do this thing this week, whether it is writing a letter, inviting a friend over, or baking some cookies!

Remind your child of the following truth: "He will not leave you or forget you" (Deuteronomy 31:8). **ASK:** How does the man in this story act like God?

Read the story directly from the Bible (Luke 14:16-24) while your child draws a picture of their favorite party food.

ASK: If you were going to have a big party, what kind of people would you invite? What kind of people did the man invite? What kind of people does God invite to be His friend?

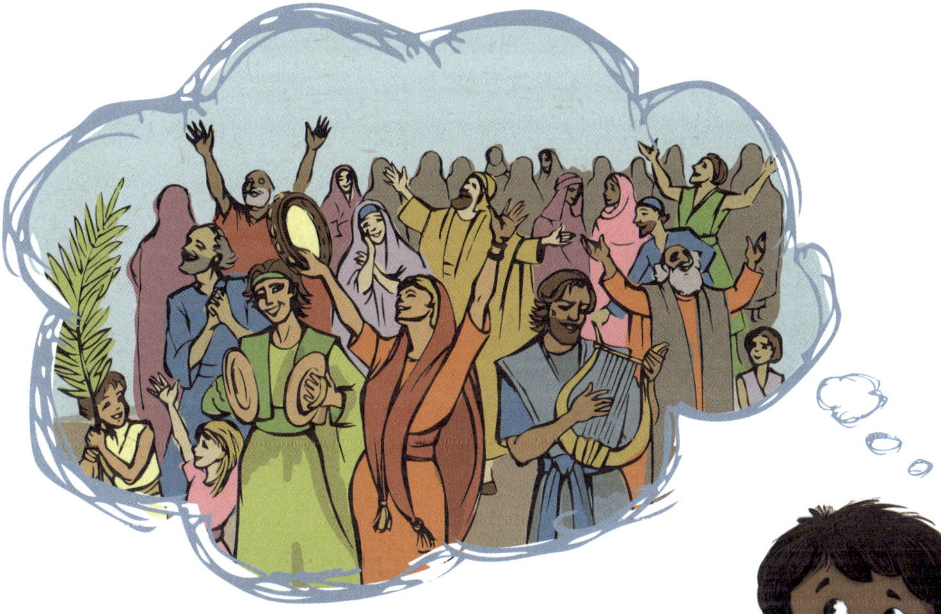

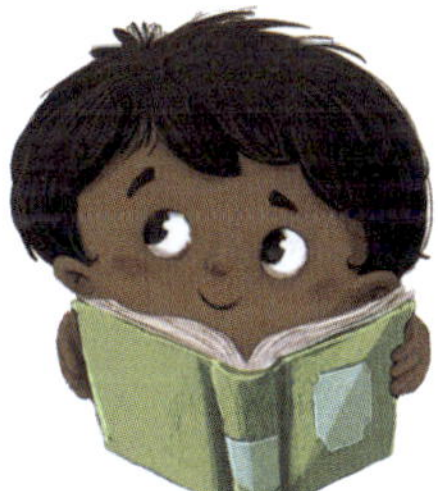

Prayer

Dear God, thank You that we are all special to You, whether we are poor, sick, or don't have any big problems. Help us to treat others the way You treat us. Amen.

Jesus Heals a Blind Man

After Jesus said this, He spit on the ground and made some mud with it and put the mud on the man's eyes. **JOHN 9:6**

One day, Jesus met a man who had been blind for his whole life. Jesus cared for the man and wanted to heal him. So He did something terribly gross: He spit into the dirt to make some mud and then put it on the man's eyes. Then He told the man to go wash off the spit-mud. The man obeyed, and he was healed. For the first time in his life, he could see!

Have your child draw a picture of mud while you read the story directly from the Bible (John 9:1-11). **ASK:** What part of this story makes you happy? Does any of it make you sad?

Tie a piece of clothing or a blindfold over your child's eyes. Have your child try to walk around a bit. **ASK:** How does that make you feel? Do you think you would like to live like that? How do you think the blind man felt when Jesus made him better?

Go into a room with no natural light and shut the door. **ASK:** Are you scared? Would you be scared if you always had to be in the dark like the blind man did? Come back into the light. Read Psalm 23:4: "Even if I walk through a very dark valley, I will not be afraid, because you are with me." **SAY:** We don't have to be afraid, because God is with us. The blind man learned that Jesus loved him very much and Jesus loves us just as much!

You will need a piece of paper, tape, and a pair of scissors. Follow the directions below to make a simple paper lantern. Read Psalm 18:28: "Lord, You give light to my lamp. My God brightens the darkness around me." **SAY:** When we are with God, we don't have to be afraid, because God can brighten the darkness, just like He turned the blind man's darkness into light. Let's keep this lantern close by to remind us that Jesus brightens the darkness around us.

LANTERN DIRECTIONS: Fold a piece of paper in half. Use scissors to make several slits starting at the fold—they should be parallel lines that are all perpendicular to the fold. Don't slice all the way to the other end. Open up the paper and turn it into a tube, with the slits going from top to bottom. Secure with tape.

Together, think of at least five things that you are so happy you can see. (rainbows, parents, flowers, etc) Thank God for each of those items and the fact that you can see them.

Prayer

Thank You, God, for loving the blind man so much You wanted to heal him. Thank You for being powerful enough to make him better. You are so amazing, and we love You! Amen.

Jesus Heals a Lame Man

Immediately the paralyzed man stood up, took his mat, and walked out while everyone was watching him. MARK 2:12

One day Jesus was teaching in a house, and there were so many people in the house that no one could get in or out. It was very squishy. But some people had a friend they really wanted to get to Jesus. So they went up on the roof, cut a hole, and lowered the guy down on a mat. This man's legs didn't work, so he couldn't walk. Jesus cared for the man and wanted to heal him. So He told him to get up and walk, and just like that, the man was all better.

Have your child draw a picture of the lame man's empty mat while reading the story from the Bible (Mark 2:1-12). **ASK:** What part of this story makes you happy? Does any of it make you sad?

Try doing a couple normal activities without legs. For example, if it's bedtime, get changed without standing, or if it's mealtime, try to go wash hands without using your legs. **SAY:** Our legs are pretty important! What do you think the lame man did all day when he couldn't use his legs? How do you think he felt when Jesus healed him?

Think of one family member or friend who deals with knee problems or other foot/leg problems (bunions, arthritis, etc.). **ASK:** Do you think that God could make their legs better? He sure could. Do you think we should ask Him right now? Pray together, asking that God would provide relief and even heal their legs entirely.

SAY: The Bible says that amazing things will happen when God comes to save His people. Read the prophecy from Isaiah 35:6: "Crippled people will jump like deer, and those who can't talk now will shout with joy. Water will flow in the desert, and streams will flow in the dry land." **SAY:** Those amazing things are called "miracles," and they are things that only God can do. What other things would be a miracle? Thank God for how amazing and powerful He is.

Together, think of at least five things that you like to do with your legs. Thank God for each of those activities and the fact that you can do them.

Prayer

Thank You, God, for loving the lame man so much that You wanted to heal him. Thank You for being powerful enough to make him better. You are so amazing, and we love You! Amen.

Jesus Heals Ten Lepers

When Jesus saw the men, He said, "Go and show yourselves to the priests." As the ten men were going, they were healed. LUKE 17:14

One day Jesus was walking in the country, and ten sick men called out to him, "Jesus! Have pity on us!" They wanted Jesus to heal them, because the sickness they had was so terrible that no one would touch them anymore. No hugs from their moms, no high fives from their friends, not even a touch on the head. These men hoped so much that Jesus would decide to heal them. And you know what? Jesus loved these men SO much, and He knew that no one else had loved them in a long time. So He healed them! He just said to them, "Go! Show the others that you are healed!" They did, and they were healed.

Have your child draw a picture of a sick person's face while you read the story from the Bible (Luke 17:11-19). **ASK:** What part of this story makes you happy? Does any of it make you sad?

With your child, act out a sickness—coughing, throwing up, having no voice, itching, whatever you can think of. **ASK:** What do you think it would be like to be sick ALL the time? Would you enjoy that? Leprosy was a terrible disease, and you could never get better from it. How do you think the lepers felt when Jesus healed them? Read another story of Jesus healing a leper: Mark 1:40-42.

SAY: It says that Jesus was filled with compassion. What is compassion? (loving someone so much that you want to help them) Pray that your family would be like Jesus—full of compassion.

Read Luke 17:15-19. **ASK:** Why do you think only one guy came back to say thank you? Do you think Jesus likes it when we say thank you? Let's think of five things that we love that we can thank God for right now.

Think of one family member or friend who is sick. **ASK:** Do you think that God could make them better? He sure could. Do you think we should ask Him right now? Pray together, asking that God would provide relief and even heal them entirely.

Prayer

Thank You, God, for loving the lame man so much that You wanted to heal him. Thank You for being powerful enough to make him better. You are so amazing, and we love You! Amen.

Jesus Raises Lazarus

So then Jesus said plainly, "Lazarus is dead. And I am glad for your sakes I was not there so that you may believe. But let's go to him now." **JOHN 11:14-15**

This week we'll be going through the whole story bit by bit. This story will probably open up a lot of questions about life, death, and heaven with your child. I encourage you to be honest with them, answering questions truthfully and biblically. When you don't know the answer, seek it together by bringing your questions to the Lord and asking Him to help you understand.

Read John 11:1, 4-6. **ASK:** What would you do if you were Jesus and your friend was sick? Do you know any sick people?

Read John 11:17. **SAY:** This means that by the time Jesus got all the way over to His friend's house, His friend Lazarus had died, and they had buried him four days ago. How would you feel if someone you knew died and you would never see them again? Read John 11:32-36. **ASK:** How did Jesus feel when He found out about Lazarus's death? How do you think He feels when other people in the world die?

Draw a picture of the story while reading John 11:38-44. **ASK:** How does this part of the story make you feel? Why do YOU think Jesus made Lazarus alive again? (A clue is in verse 42.)

Read John 11:23-26. **SAY:** Here Jesus says that when we believe in Him, we will live forever with Him in heaven. What do you know about heaven? Allow your child to dream a bit about what heaven will be like. There are many wonderful picture books on heaven, which you can use if your child is extra curious. **SAY:** Jesus asks Martha if she believes Him—do YOU believe what Jesus says in these verses?

Act out the last part of the story with your child (John 11:38-44). **ASK:** What is your favorite part of the story? Did you know that Jesus loves YOU just as much as Jesus loved Lazarus and his sisters? How does that make you feel?

Prayer

Thank You, God, for showing everyone how amazing You are. Thank You for loving Mary and Martha and Lazarus, and that You are powerful enough to bring people back from the dead. Amen.

Jesus Meets a Woman at a Well

When a Samaritan woman came to the well to get some water, Jesus said to her, "Please give me a drink." **JOHN 4:1-42**

One day Jesus and His disciples were walking through Samaria, which was a place that Jewish people didn't like to go. They considered the Samaritans their enemies. But Jesus stopped at a well to talk to a lady who had no friends. He told her that He loved everyone and had come to give them eternal life. She was so excited that she told everyone in her town about Jesus' great love.

Act out the story with your child. **ASK:** Why do you think Jesus stopped to talk with the lady? What did He ask for? What do you think He really wanted?

Have your child draw a picture of a bucket of water while you read the story straight from John 4:5-14. **ASK:** What's your favorite part of the story? Why?

Read John 4:9. **SAY:** Jesus loves everyone. Jesus even loves people whom others may not like a whole lot—like the Samaritans. Have you ever had a hard time getting along with someone? Do you think Jesus wants you to love people, even when you don't play together well? Let's pray that you would show Jesus' love.

Read John 4:28-30, 39-42. **SAY:** Because Jesus stopped and showed love to one lonely lady, a whole town full of people came to believe that He is the Savior of the world. Let's think of one lonely person that we could show love to this week. (Write down their name and how you're going to show love.) Perhaps by showing Jesus' love to him or her, another whole town full of people will come to believe in Jesus!

Get a cup of water, then read John 4:10-15. **ASK:** If we drink this cup of water now, will we be able to go through the rest of our lives without drinking? What about if we drink a glass of milk? No matter what we drink, we will always need more drinks to keep us alive. Jesus is talking about giving us something that will fill up our souls so we never want for anything more—because we are filled with Jesus' love.

Prayer

Dear Jesus, thank You for showing love to the woman at the well. Teach us to show love to those who are unlovable. Amen.

Jesus Meets Zacchaeus

When Jesus came to that place, he looked up and said to him, "Zacchaeus, hurry and come down! I must stay at your house today." **LUKE 19:1-10**

Zacchaeus was a very small man with a very small heart. He took money from people through taxes and kept a lot of it for himself. But when Jesus came through town, Zacchaeus climbed a tree in order to see him. And when Jesus came by the tree, He asked Zacchaeus to come down and invited Himself over! When he learned about Jesus' love, Zacchaeus's heart grew to love God and people.

Measure how tall your child is against a doorjamb. **ASK:** How tall do you think Zacchaeus was? No matter how tall we are, Jesus loves us. He loves you when you're this tall, and He'll love you when you're taller than me! How big do you think your heart is? No matter how much love you have, Jesus loves you more!

Read the story from a children's Bible or from Luke 19:1-10 while your child draws a picture of a tree. **ASK:** What is your favorite part of this story? Why?

Act out the story with your child. **ASK:** Did you learn something new from the story today? What was it?

Pretend to go for a walk with your child. Suddenly, stop and look up. **SAY:** Pretend you are Jesus—would you have stopped to talk to the guy nobody else liked? Why do you think Jesus looked up and talked to Zacchaeus when he was in the tree?

Read Luke 19:8. **ASK:** What did Zacchaeus do? Together with your child, pray and listen for God's ideas on how you could respond to God's love. It might be something like giving some of your possessions to the poor, or it might be something else. Ask God to give you and your child creativity, be open to His response, and then obey!

Prayer

Dear Jesus, thank You for showing your deep love to Zacchaeus and for reminding us that You love us, no matter how big we are or who we are. Help us to love like You. Amen.

Jesus Visits Mary and Martha

"Only one thing is important. Mary has chosen the better thing, and it will never be taken away from her." LUKE 10:42

Mary and Martha were sisters, and they were both friends with Jesus. One day, Martha was scurrying around getting everything ready for Jesus, while Mary was sitting with Jesus and listening to Him teach. Martha was really annoyed that Mary was just sitting there, so she complained to Jesus. But Jesus said something surprising to her; He said it was even MORE important for them to listen to His words than it was to clean the house and cook food for Him.

Read the paraphrase then act out the story together. **ASK:** Why do you think Jesus wanted Mary and Martha to listen to Him?

Practice turning on your listening ears because it's time to listen to God! One way we can hear God is through the Bible. Read Joshua 1:9 with your child. **ASK:** What do you think God wants to say to us through this Bible verse?

Read the story directly from the Bible (Luke 10:38-42) or a children's Bible while your child draws a picture of a head with ears.

Time to listen to God! Read 1 John 4:19 with your child. **ASK:** What do you think God wants to say to us through this Bible verse?

Today we're going to listen to God in a different way—if our hearts are open to Him, God will often speak to us directly. Help your child get into a comfortable listening position, and then pray the following prayer together. **SAY:** Jesus, please help me to listen to You today. Help my heart and mind to be quiet so I can hear You. Jesus, what would You like to say to us today?

Once your child is ready, have them report back what Jesus said to them. Be prepared to be surprised, but if they don't "hear" anything, remind them that as we keep our ears and hearts open, God will speak.

Prayer

Thank You, God, for loving me. Please help me to learn to make my body be still and my thoughts be quiet so that I can hear You speaking to me. Amen.

Jesus Is Worshiped by Mary

Mary brought in a pint of very expensive perfume made from pure nard. She poured the perfume on Jesus' feet, and then she wiped his feet with her hair. **JOHN 12:3**

Jesus was visiting with Mary and Martha again. While Jesus was sitting at the table, Mary took a bottle of very expensive perfume and poured it all over His feet. Then she wiped His feet with her hair. The others at the table thought this was totally crazy, but Jesus said what she had done was beautiful.

Read the paraphrase then act out the story together. **ASK:** Why do you think Mary poured the perfume on Jesus' feet?

SAY: We can show Jesus that we love Him by serving each other. Let's think about a way that you and I can serve each other right now. (You could help each other get a drink of water or you could help your child put PJs on or your child could help you get your bed ready for bedtime. Let your child be creative!)

Read the story directly from the Bible (John 12:1-3) or from a children's Bible while your child draws a picture of an expensive bottle of perfume.

SAY: The Bible says that the whole house was filled with the fragrance of the perfume. What kinds of things does our house smell like? Together, see if you can find something that smells lovely—like a new bar of soap, essential oils, or a bottle of vanilla. Talk about what it might be like to have your whole house smell like this because someone was covered in it.

Using the sweet-smelling item from yesterday (or something different), plan to give it to someone as a way of serving them. Write a little note that says, "We can love Jesus by serving you" (or something to that effect). Plan to deliver it within the next 24 hours so you don't forget!

Prayer

Thank You, God, for loving me.
Help me to show love to You by loving and serving other people! Amen.

Jesus Rides into Jerusalem

They brought the donkey and the colt to Jesus and laid their coats on them, and Jesus sat on them. **MATTHEW 21:7**

Jesus came with His friends to Jerusalem, but before they went into town, He sent two of His friends to get a donkey. When they brought the donkey back, they put their coats on the donkey and Jesus sat on top. This is how He rode into Jerusalem, the most important city around. A very large crowd came into town and put their coats on the road. They also got tree branches and put them on the road for the donkey and Jesus to ride on. Then they shouted, "Hosanna in the highest! Blessed is He who comes in the name of the Lord!"

Act out the story with your child using yourselves, stuffed animals, or dolls. **ASK:** Why do you think the people got so excited? What is your favorite part of this story? Why?

ASK: If Jesus walked into this room right now, what words would you say to Him? (wait for answers) The people in the story shouted "Hosanna!" which means "hooray! We are saved!" Let's practice shouting "hosanna" to Jesus right now!

ASK: If you were a king or queen coming into a city, how would you like to come into town? Would you ride a donkey, or would you come on something fancier?

FOR AGES 5+: Did you know that a man named Zechariah knew that Jesus was going to ride into Jerusalem on a donkey (instead of a horse or a chariot) way before Jesus was even born? Read Zechariah 9:9. How do you think Zechariah knew this would happen? (God told him) That verse was a clue to the people in Jesus' time that He was going to be the King of the whole world. Do you think that Jesus is a good King?

Read Matthew 21:15-16. **SAY:** When the leaders heard the kids praising Jesus in the temple, Jesus tells them that God loves it when kids sing praise to Him. Let's sing a song of praise to God right now, because we know that He will love it! (Sing one of your child's favorite songs about Jesus.)

Use a piece of paper and crayons to trace your child's hands. Help them cut the hands out. Wave the paper hands like palm branches. Have your child repeat the words of the people's praises after you: "Hosanna to the Son of David! Blessed is He who comes in the name of the Lord! Hosanna in the highest! Hosanna!"

Prayer

Thank You, Jesus, for loving us and coming to earth to be the King of our hearts. Help us to always love You and be excited by You, just like the people in this story were excited to see You. Amen.

Jesus Dies for Us

Short Edition, for Ages 2/3

When they came to a place called the Skull, the soldiers crucified Jesus and the criminals—one on His right and the other on His left. Jesus said, "Father, forgive them, because they don't know what they are doing." **LUKE 23:33-34**

Some bad guys didn't like Jesus, so they decided that they would try to get Him in trouble. They arrested Him and got everyone to be mad at him, then they sent Him to die on a cross. Even though Jesus hadn't done anything wrong, He still took the punishment. After He died, His friends rolled up His body in some cloth and laid Him in a cave, with a big rock over the door. Three days later, some of His friends came by to put perfume on His body, except that it wasn't there! Instead, an angel stood by the cave and told them that Jesus was alive again. They were so surprised and also very excited, so they ran off to tell all their other friends the good news.

Read the paraphrase then act it out with your child. (NOTE: This story can be quite horrifying to an imaginative or empathetic child. If your child has questions, answer them as best you can, and share your own feelings about Jesus' death with them. If you're fairly matter of fact about it, your child will be as well.) **ASK:** How do you think His friends felt after He died? Why? Would you have felt that way?

SAY: Way back in the beginning of the Bible, we learned about Adam and Eve's sin and how there was a punishment for it. The punishment was that people were always separated from God, because He's perfect and we're not. Jesus took the punishment for us, so now we can be with God! Let's thank Jesus.

Read the story from a simple children's Bible while your child draws a picture of a cross.

Together, try to push a wall as if you are pushing the rock away from Jesus's tomb. **SAY:** This is what it would be like for just one person to try to move the rock in front of the cave. How do you think the angel did it? Who made Jesus come back to life?

ASK: Let's use our imaginations. What do you think Jesus did when He first came back to life? Where did He go? What was the first word He said?

Prayer

Thank You, Jesus, for dying and coming back to life. You are really amazing! Help us to understand what this means for our lives. Amen.

Jesus Dies for Us

Extended Edition, for Ages 4+

When they came to a place called the Skull, the soldiers crucified Jesus and the criminals—one on His right and the other on His his left. Jesus said, "Father, forgive them, because they don't know what they are doing." **LUKE 23:33-34**

NOTE: We will be slowly going through the Easter story, with 10 installments over two weeks. There are several schools of thought on whether or not preschoolers are ready to hear the Easter story. As it is the central tenet of our faith, I think they need to hear it. In a culture where it's normal for a preschooler to watch movies about superheroes (where there's a decent amount of death and destruction), I think it's quite appropriate for them to talk about the death of Christ. They won't understand the full significance of His death and the sadness that it brought His followers, but that's no reason to avoid teaching about Jesus' sacrifice for us. Let them hear it, let them be moved by the sadness of His friends, and let them rejoice all the more in the resurrection because they have seen what the alternative is!

Jesus washes His friends' feet: Read John 13:4-14.
Now, do as Jesus commands and wash your child's feet—in a tub, a sink, or just with wet cloths. Allow your child to wash your feet as well. **SAY:** How did you feel when you washed my feet? How does

it make you feel that Jesus would wash our dirty feet? Why do you think Jesus wants us to do this?

The Last Supper: Read Mark 14:22-24.

ASK: Did you know that Jesus came to rescue us? Do you know why we need to be rescued? We need rescuing because we do bad things, called sin, and those bad things keep us from God. Jesus wants to rescue us from our sin—to forgive us and to help us change. Think of one or two things today for which you need forgiveness and ask Jesus to rescue you from that sin.

Jesus prays in the garden: Read Mark 14:32-42.

SAY: Jesus was very sad, because He knew that all our badness was going to go into His heart. How does it make you feel that all the badness in your heart had to go into Jesus' heart? That because of the bad things you and I have done, Jesus had to be punished? Do you think that's fair? I don't think that's fair. But because Jesus loves us SO much, that's what He chose to do. Let's thank Him right now for being so wonderful to us!

Jesus is arrested: Read Mark 14:43-50.

ASK: Why did Peter slice off the man's ear? (because he was afraid, and he was trying to protect Jesus) What would you have done if someone came to arrest your best friend? Even though Jesus could have stopped them from arresting Him, He didn't. Why not?

Jesus' trial: Read Mark 14:53-64.

ASK: Do you think Jesus was afraid to die? Can you think of a reason why the leaders would hate Jesus so much? (they were afraid of Him, afraid of the Romans, they didn't like people who were different, they were jealous) It's a terrible thing that these leaders hated Jesus. Yet God used them in His great rescue plan. Jesus had to die, and He used these mean and jealous leaders to make His plan work. But Jesus didn't hate the leaders back. He wants us to love people who hurt us. Let's pray that we would be able to love those who make us feel bad.

Jesus is crucified: Read Mark 15:25-34.

ASK: Do you know why Jesus stayed on that cross? It was love. Who does Jesus love? He loves YOU. _______ (name), Jesus loves YOU so much that He chose to take the punishment for the wrong things YOU'VE done. How does that make you feel? Would you like to say something to Jesus?

Jesus dies and is buried: Read Mark 15:37-46.

SAY: How do you think Jesus' friends felt as they buried His body in the tomb? How would you feel if your best friend died? I think they were probably terribly sad. But did you know that the story doesn't end here? Jesus had to die to take the punishment for our sin, but He also had another thing He had to do!

Jesus' body is gone: Read Mark 16:1-8.

ASK: Wow, wasn't that a surprise?! How would you feel if you saw a huge, shiny angel? What did you think of the angels' news? Do you think you would have believed the angel if you had been one of those women?

Jesus talks to Mary: Read John 20:11-18.

SAY: Mary was so excited to see Jesus, because she thought He was going to be dead forever. But Jesus is God's Son, and He couldn't stay dead—He had to come back to life so that death could come untrue—so that all the people who love Him can eventually came back to life too. Do you or I know anyone who has died that someday will come back to life? How do you think we will feel when we see them? Will we feel like Mary did—excited and joyful and a little bit scared? Or something else?

Jesus appears to His friends: Read Luke 24:36-43.

SAY: Touch me—am I real? Jesus' friends thought He wasn't really there, but when they touched him, they felt that He was just as real as you or me. But the Bible tells us that Jesus' body was not only real, it was better than real—it could never get sick or hurt or die ever again. The great news is that someday, Jesus will give us bodies just like that too! How do you feel about that? Let's thank God for His amazing rescue plan!

Jesus Meets Friends on the Road

That same day two of Jesus' followers were going to a town named Emmaus, about seven miles from Jerusalem. They were talking about everything that had happened. **LUKE 24:13-14**

Two of Jesus' friends were going for a walk when a stranger joined them. They told the stranger all about what had happened with Jesus—that He was so wonderful but bad people had put him on a cross to die and that some of Jesus' friends said He was alive again. The stranger explained lots of things to them and told them why it was important for Jesus to die and come back to life. These two men invited the stranger for supper. When He was at the table with them, He took bread, gave thanks, broke it, and began to give it to them. They suddenly realized that the man was actually JESUS! But just as soon as they figured it out, Jesus disappeared.

Read the paraphrase then act out the story with your child or use stuffed animals.

ASK: Why do you think the two men didn't recognize Jesus right away? How would you recognize Jesus? What do you think He looks like?

Have your child draw a picture of three people as you read the story from Luke 24:13-32 or from a children's Bible.

ASK: What did Jesus' friends do when they recognized Him? (hint, see verses 33-35) Let's try running around and telling everyone around the great news! (Jesus is alive!)

You will need a piece of paper and a pencil. Trace your child's footprint and write the following verse inside the print: "I call you friends" (John 15:15). Practice saying it together.

Prayer

Jesus, that was a pretty neat thing You did when You showed up to explain all about Your death to Your friends and then let them see who You really were later. Please help us to recognize Your presence in our lives. Amen.

Jesus Gives the Great Commission

"Go and make followers of all people in the world. Baptize them in the name of the Father and the Son and the Holy Spirit. Teach them to obey everything that I have taught you, and I will be with you always, even until the end of this age." **MATTHEW 28:19-20**

After He came back to life, Jesus told His friends to meet on a mountain. Jesus met them there and told them they had a new job to do! Their job was to tell everyone they met about Jesus' love, teaching them about God the Father, God's Son Jesus, and the Holy Spirit. They were to teach everyone how to follow and love Jesus. And Jesus promised to be with them always, even if they couldn't see Him.

Read and act out the story with your child. **ASK:** What do you think about Jesus's instructions?

You will need a map (physical or digital) or a globe. Show your child some of the parts of the earth and talk about how God loves everyone in the whole world and wants them to love Him too.

SAY: Jesus gave His friends a special message to tell the world. Do you remember what that special message is? (At a loss? Try "Jesus wants to be your friend forever" or some variant of that message.) Let's practice telling each other that special message.

SAY: There are many different ways that we can tell people about Jesus' love. We can send emails or letters, tell people on the phone, or just shout it out loud! Let's pick one way and try it out today.

Read Matthew 28:16-20 while your child draws a picture of the earth.

Prayer

Thank You, Jesus, for loving us! Help us to share Your love with everyone we meet. Amen.

Jesus Goes to Heaven

After He said this, as they were watching, He was lifted up, and a cloud hid Him from their sight. **ACTS 1:9**

After His resurrection, Jesus' friends were still expecting him to kick out the bad king and sit on His throne. But instead, He told them they were going to be making disciples now. He also said that He would send a special helper to help them. This would be the Holy Spirit. Then, as Jesus' friends stood watching from a hill-side, Jesus went back up into heaven. Up, up, up He went as His friends stretched their necks to see where He was going. Where was He going? Two angels came to talk to the confused friends and told them that Jesus was going to prepare a place for them and for us! One day, He will return to earth to be our King.

Act out the story with your child. If you have access to dolls or stuffed animals, use them as all the other people watching Jesus go and/or as the angels.

Read Acts 1:6-11 while your child draws a picture of the sky and clouds. **ASK:** Where did Jesus go? Why did He go? How do you think His friends felt as they watched Him go up into the sky?

Read John 14:1-4. **ASK:** How many rooms are in our home? Go through and count the rooms in your home and talk about the purpose of each room. Jesus said that He was going to prepare a place in His house with many rooms. How big do you think Jesus' house is? What do you think Jesus' house is like? What do you think will be the best part of Jesus' house?

ASK: What part of this story makes you happy? Sad? Mad? Jesus said He would never leave them, but He went up to heaven. So what do you think it means that He will never leave us?

Help your child memorize the following verse: "So go and make followers of all people in the world" (Matthew 28:19). **SAY:** When Jesus went up to heaven, He gave all of His friends (including us) a special job—we are supposed to "make disciples," which means that we need to help others learn to follow Jesus. Today let's pray that God will give us courage to tell others about Jesus' love.

Prayer

Dear Jesus, thank You for going up to heaven to prepare a special place for us! You love us so much, and we love You too. Help us to do the job that You asked us to do—to go everywhere and tell everyone the happy news about Your love. Amen.

Jesus' Spirit Arrives

They were all filled with the Holy Spirit, and they began to speak different languages by the power the Holy Spirit was giving them. **ACTS 2:1-6**

After Jesus went up to heaven, His friends gathered all together. One day, the house they were in was filled with the sound of a noisy wind, even with no windows open! As Jesus' friends looked around, they saw something that looked like fire on each person's head. This was the Holy Spirit. He was coming to fill them up with God's power and give them courage to tell others about God's love. As soon as this happened, they all ran outside and began telling everyone about Jesus. There were people from many different countries in the city at that time, and Jesus' friends found themselves suddenly able to speak in each of the different languages, so that every person in the crowd could hear about Jesus.

Read the paraphrase together then act out the story with your child. **SAY:** Pentecost is the first birthday of the Church because it's when Jesus' friends received the Holy Spirit and started telling the whole world about His death and resurrection. That was over 2000 years ago, and now there are millions of people all over the world who love Jesus. Together, we are called the Church. Let's sing Happy Birthday to the Church as a way to celebrate! (If you know how to sing "Happy Birthday" in another language, this would be a good time to teach your kids.)

Read the story out of Acts 2:1-6. **ASK:** What languages can you speak? Try a few words in another language, like French or Spanish. What did Jesus' friends do when they discovered they could speak other languages? (The answer is found in Acts 2:11.) One of the gifts that the Holy Spirit gives is the ability to tell other people about Jesus in a language that we haven't learned. Let's pray for people in other parts of the world that someone would come to them and teach them about Jesus in their own language.

Read Acts 2:2. **ASK:** What do you think a "violent wind" would sound like? Try blowing as hard as you can to make a sound that can fill your whole house. **ASK:** Where do you think the wind came from?

Pretend to light a fire together (or you can light a candle). **SAY:** How would it feel to have your body covered in fire? Can you think of another story in the Bible where there was a fire that didn't burn anything up? (Hint, look in Exodus!) That was also God's Spirit!

Draw a flame on a piece of paper, and tape it to your child's back to remind them that anyone who is a child of God is filled with the Holy Spirit, just like the disciples. It just might not be quite as outwardly obvious as having a flame of fire on your head!

Prayer

God, thank You so much for sending the gift of the Holy Spirit to the disciples and to me. Help me to love You more and more each day. Amen.

A Lame Man Is Healed

But Peter said, "I don't have any silver or gold, but I do have something else I can give you. By the power of Jesus Christ from Nazareth, stand up and walk!" **ACTS 3:6**

Peter and John went to the temple together one day, and they met a man who sat in front of the gates every day. This man was crippled, which means he couldn't walk. He asked Peter and John for some money. Peter and John decided they wouldn't give him any money this time, but they would give him something much better. Peter told him to get up and walk, in the name of Jesus! The man jumped right up and began to walk. He went with them and began running and jumping and praising God. Everyone who saw him was amazed. The Holy Spirit gave Peter the power to heal just like Jesus did when He lived on earth.

Act out the story with your child, using dolls as extra characters if available. **ASK:** What is your favorite part of this story? Why?

Read the story out of the Bible (Acts 3:1-11) while your child draws a picture of a guy sitting. **ASK:** Did you learn anything different in the story today?

ASK: Do you remember another story like this in the Bible? Check out Mark 2:1-4, 12. **ASK:** Who did the first miracle of healing a crippled man? (Jesus) Why do you think Peter and John were also able to heal a crippled man? (They did it in the name of Jesus Christ; they were empowered by the Holy Spirit who had just come to be with them; they had the Spirit of God giving them power, so they were able to do a lot of miracles like Jesus did!)

Pretend that you are the crippled man. Try to do some normal activities without using your legs. How does it feel? Then, say "in the name of Jesus Christ, walk!" and jump up! Do all kinds of things with your legs—jumping, walking, dancing, karate kicks—whatever fills you and your child with joy.

Read John 14:12. **SAY:** What kind of works did Jesus do? (healing, loving, feeding many people, bringing people back to life) Jesus said that anyone who believes in Him will be able to do even greater things than He did! That's because we have the Holy Spirit filling us with courage and power.

Prayer

God, thank You for the amazing miracles that Jesus' friends were able to do because Your Spirit filled them with the power of God. Help me to trust in Your Spirit to help me do things that seem impossible! Amen.

Tabitha Is Healed

Peter sent everyone out of the room and kneeled and prayed. Then he turned to the body and said, "Tabitha, stand up." She opened her eyes, and when she saw Peter, she sat up. **ACTS 9:40**

There was a lady named Tabitha who helped a lot of people, and she was very much loved. She would sew beautiful clothes for people who were poor. But then she got sick and died. Her friends were very sad, so they called Peter and asked him to bring her back to life. He walked into the room where her body was and prayed. Then he said "Tabitha, get up." She came back to life, opened her eyes, and popped up! Because the Holy Spirit worked in Peter to do amazing miracles, many people believed in God.

Act out this story with your child. As you do, talk about the different emotions the people in the story might have experienced, such as love, sadness, fear, courage, and joy.

Read the story right out of Acts 9:36-42 while your child draws a picture of a piece of clothing. **ASK:** What is your favorite part of this story?

SAY: There are two people in this story that the Holy Spirit helped to do wonderful things. Who are they? (Peter and Tabitha) What special job did the Holy Spirit help Tabitha do? (see verses 36, 39 for answers) Let's ask the Holy Spirit to help us know what our special jobs are and to help us do them.

Pick out a few pieces from your child's wardrobe and find out where they are made. **SAY:** Tabitha was a person who helped poor people by sewing clothes for them. Today, the people who sew our clothes are usually poor because they don't get paid very much. See these tags? These clothes were made in ______________ (Bangladesh, India, Thailand, etc). We need to pray for these people that someone like Tabitha would help them in their need. We also need to pray that the Holy Spirit would show us how WE can help. Spend time praying together.

Read Acts 9:40. **ASK:** What did Peter do before he was able to bring Tabitha back to life? We need to learn to talk to God about everything and to listen to Him. As we learn to do that better, we may be able to do amazing miracles through the Holy Spirit just like Peter. Let's talk to God right now.

Prayer

Thank You, God, for doing something so amazing and bringing Tabitha back to life. Help me to be like Peter who, through Your power, brought Tabitha back to life. And help me to be like Tabitha who was always helping people in need. Amen.

Peter Escapes from Jail

Peter was kept in jail, but the church prayed earnestly to God for him. **ACTS 12:5**

The king of Israel didn't like Peter and his friends very much because he was afraid of the Holy Spirit's power working in them. So the king arrested Peter and put him in jail. One night, while his friends prayed for him, an angel came to Peter and helped him escape from jail. Peter went to the house where his friends were, and they were so surprised to see him that they almost forgot to let him in the door! In the morning, no one at the jail could figure out where Peter had gone, because God had set him free.

Act out the story with your child or draw a picture of the story together. **ASK:** What do you find most surprising about this story?

Read the story out of Acts 12:4-10 while your child draws a picture of a jail. **ASK:** Why do you think Peter thought the angel wasn't real, that he was just dreaming? Have you ever seen an angel or something that others might think was just a dream?

Play a short game of "follow the leader" with your child while pretending that one of you is Peter in jail and one of you is the angel who says, "follow me." **ASK:** What would you think if an angel came to you and said to follow him?

Read Acts 12:11-17 then act out or talk about this part of the story together. **ASK:** Why do you think the people were so surprised to see Peter?

If you are able, spend a couple minutes on the computer before doing this devotion. Go to www.persecution.net and look at the "Persecution and Prayer Alert" for news about persecution of Christians in other countries. Find one that you feel is appropriate for your child and use it to pray specifically.

SAY: The Bible doesn't say that Peter was freed from prison just because the church prayed for him, but it does say that God listens to our prayers. There are many pastors and Christians that are in jail in other countries right now. Let's pray for people in__________ (country) who are being hurt and put in jail by people who don't understand God's love.

Prayer

Thank You, God, for setting Peter free from jail so he could continue to teach others about You! Help us to remember that You really do answer prayers, even when they seem impossible. Amen.

Saul Escapes from Damascus

One night some followers of Saul helped him leave the city by lowering him in a basket through an opening in the city wall. **ACTS 9:25**

Saul (who we later call Paul) was a bad man, but Jesus changed his heart and he started to tell everyone around how amazing Jesus is. Some people didn't like that, so they made a plan to hurt him. His friends found out about the plan to hurt Saul, and they snuck him out of the city by putting him in a basket and lowering him down from the city wall in the middle of the night!

Review the story with your child, either by acting it out together or telling it in a dramatic voice. **ASK:** What's your favorite part of this story?

Have your child draw a picture of Saul in a basket while reading Acts 9:19-25 straight from the Bible. **ASK:** Why do you think those people wanted to hurt Saul?

Have your child sit in a laundry basket while you either wiggle it around or pick it up and carry it around. **ASK:** How do you think Saul felt when they were lowering him in a basket through an opening in the wall? Do you think he was scared? Why or why not?

Read Acts 9:22. **ASK:** What was Saul telling people? Why was he telling people that? Have you ever told somebody that?

If you are able, spend a couple minutes on the computer before doing this devotion. Go to www.persecution.net and look at the "Persecution and Prayer Alert" for news about persecution of Christians in other countries. Find one that you feel is appropriate for your child and use it to pray specifically.

SAY: Let's pray for people in ______ (country) who are being hurt and put in jail by people who don't understand God's love. Pray that they would be strong in the Lord, that people would come to know Jesus' love through their love, and that God would protect them from harm.

Prayer

Thank You, God, for protecting Saul from the people that wanted to hurt him. Help us to be bold in telling others about Jesus, just like Saul. Amen.

Paul in a Shipwreck

The angel said, "Paul, do not be afraid. You must stand before Caesar. And God has promised you that He will save the lives of everyone sailing with you." **ACTS 27:24**

Paul had been arrested in Jerusalem and was being sent to Rome to stand trial before Caesar. To get there, they had to take a boat, but they had quite an adventure on the sea! This week we'll be adventuring with Paul, hearing the whole story. After each reading, feel free to act it out with your child, have them draw a picture of the story, or just discuss it together.

Read Acts 27:13-26. **SAY:** Paul told them before they started sailing that they would have a shipwreck, but they didn't listen. Was he mad at them for not listening? How did he treat them? Let's ask God to help us treat people with respect even when they are rude to us.

Read Acts 27:27-38. **SAY:** It sounds like all the sailors are very afraid. Why is Paul being so brave? (In his letters he explains that it comes from the grace he found in the Holy Spirit.) How would you feel if you were in the middle of the ocean in a giant storm?

Read Acts 27:39-44. **SAY:** In yesterday's story, Paul told the people on the ship that God had promised that no one would get hurt (verse 34). Did God keep His promise? Isn't it amazing that God even protected the soldiers who wanted to kill Paul and the sailors who wanted to run away? God loves everyone and has a plan for each person's life.

Read Acts 28:1-6. **SAY:** What is surprising about this story? The people from the island made a mistake in verse 6. Was Paul really a god? (no!) But God was taking care of him.

Read Acts 28:7-10. **SAY:** The man's father was quite sick, but Paul healed him. How did Paul heal him? (He prayed, and the Holy Spirit helped him.)

Prayer

Thank You, God, for showing Your awesome power to Paul and the sailors on the ship. Thank You for being a great and merciful God. Amen.

Paul and Silas in Prison

About midnight Paul and Silas were praying and singing songs to God as the other prisoners listened. **ACTS 16:25**

Paul and his friend Silas helped a girl who was sick. But there were some people who didn't want her to get well; they got angry and made Paul and Silas get arrested. While they were in jail, Paul and Silas prayed and sang to God. Suddenly the walls and the floors started to shake, the chains fell off the prisoners, and the doors fell off their hinges. It was a giant earthquake! But even though the doors were open and their chains fell off, Paul and Silas didn't run away. Rather, they stayed behind to show Jesus' love to the jailer, who knew he'd be in big trouble if the prisoners escaped. Instead, he learned of God's great love for him, and his whole family chose to follow Jesus!

Act out the story together with your child. **ASK:** What is your favorite part of the story?

Read Acts 16:23-36 from the Bible while your child draws a picture of chains.

SAY: While in jail, Paul and Silas did something strange. Instead of moaning and groaning, they prayed and sang. Why do you think

they did that? Let's pretend we're in jail right now, and we'll sing a song about Jesus together.

Sit on a bed or couch and pretend that you are in jail. **SAY:** Here comes a big earthquake! The doors are open and the chains are off. What should we do? Uh oh, here comes the man who put the chains on us. Should we beat him up and run away? If not, what should we do instead? What did Paul and Silas do?

SAY: Peter and Silas had the chance to tell the jailer about Jesus. Read the part that says what they told him (Acts 16:29-33). Is this what your household believes? Have you been baptized like the jailer and his family?

Prayer

Thank You, God, for showing Your amazing power to Paul, Silas, and the jailer. You are big enough to cause an earthquake, yet You cared so much for each person in the jailer's family. Help us to love others like You do. Amen.

Timothy Learns the Scriptures

I remember your true faith. That faith first lived in your grandmother Lois and in your mother Eunice, and I know you now have that same faith. **2 TIMOTHY 1:5**

Timothy learned all about Jesus and the Bible from his mother and grandmother. When he got a little older, he worked with a man named Paul. Together, Timothy and Paul explored much of the world, teaching everyone they met about Jesus. Because Timothy was taught the Bible when he was very young, he was able to become a leader in the church when he was still a young man.

Act out how you think Timothy would have learned from his mother and grandmother when he was a boy. Did they read him books? Tell him stories? Bring him to church? **SAY:** What do you think are the most important things that Timothy's mother taught him? What are the most important things your mother teaches you?

Read 2 Timothy 1:5; 3:14-15 aloud while your child draws a picture of a Bible. **SAY:** These verses explain that Timothy knew God's Word even when he was a very little boy. Do you know God's stories and His love?

Read 1 Timothy 4:12. **SAY:** This verse means that even though you are young, you can follow God just like an adult can. You can be the one to remind adults about faith and love! What are some things you can do to be a good example for others?

Read 1 Timothy 6:18. **SAY:** This is another thing that Timothy learned. What does this mean to you? How can you be like this verse says this week? Remember that we cannot do these things alone—we need to ask the Holy Spirit to help us!

Read 2 Timothy 1:14. The following truth has been taken from this verse: "The Holy Spirit lives in us and will help us." Practice it together with your child!

Prayer

God, thank You for all the people who teach us about You. Help me to learn about You and love You more each day! Amen

God Teaches through the Bible

The Bible says that "I will make you wise and show you where to go" **PSALM 32:8**

God has given us the Bible, which teaches us all about Him and makes us wise. This week we are going to go through a few of the most important lessons in the Bible.

Read Genesis 1:1. **ASK:** What do we learn about God from this verse? How powerful is God? How big is God? (Major point: God is amazing.)

Read Psalm 139:13-14. **ASK:** What do we learn about God from this verse? (Major point: God made me.)

Read Zephaniah 3:17. **ASK:** What do we learn about God from this verse? (Major point: God loves me.)

Read John 3:16. **ASK:** What do we learn about God from this verse? (Major point: Jesus wants to be my friend forever.)

Read Matthew 22:37-39. **ASK:** What does God teach us in this verse? (Major point: God wants us to love Him and to love others.)

Prayer

Thank You so much, God, for giving us the Bible. Help us to love reading the Bible, to think about it day and night, and to share it with others. Amen.

God Teaches through Our Parents

"I will make you wise and show you where to go." **PSALM 32:8**

One of the ways that God teaches you is by giving you parents who teach you how to follow God. This week we're going to look up some verses that talk about how God uses your parents to teach you about Him.

Read Exodus 20:12. **ASK:** What do you think it means to honor your mom and dad?

Read Deuteronomy 6:6-7. **ASK:** When are we supposed to talk about God and the Bible? With whom are we supposed to talk about God?

Read 1 John 1:9. **ASK:** Have you ever done something bad? Was I angry with you? Did I forgive you? When I forgave you, I was showing you what God is like. God doesn't like it when we do bad things, but He forgives us and helps us change.

Read 1 John 3:1 (just the first sentence). **SAY:** Close your eyes and imagine a cupcake. Now imagine that you are putting icing on your cupcake. How much are you putting on? Lots and lots, right? That's

what the word "lavished" means. Just like we lavish lots of icing onto a cupcake, God has lavished so much love on us! Now, let God's love flow through you as you have your child sit on your lap while you pretend to spread "love icing" on him/her. Have a good laugh and revel in God's immense love!

Read Ephesians 6:1. **ASK:** Why are we supposed to obey our parents? Is that hard sometimes? Let's ask God to help us obey.

Prayer

Thank You, God, for my parent(s). Thank You for giving them to me. Help my parent(s) to learn from You so that they can teach me about You. Amen.

We Love God through Prayer

Prayer is a very important way to show Jesus that we love Him, because it requires talking to Him and listening to Him. Prayer helps us develop a relationship with God. We're going to try several different prayer activities this week. Use them in your future prayer times to help your child connect with God in the way that works best for your child.

Tactile prayer: Grab a small ball or some rolled up socks and toss it to each other. Every time you catch, say a prayer!

Visual prayer: Bring some pictures to prayer time with you. These could be pictures of family, sponsor children, or almost anything. As you look at each picture, pray about it. For example, if it's a picture of your family, pray for your family. If it's a picture of a beautiful flower, thank God for doing such an amazing job of creating the flower!

Auditory prayer: Whisper/yell/use different voices during your prayers to God.

Listening prayer: Ask the following questions of God, and then have your child listen for the answer and report back to you.

A) God, is there anything today that we could thank You for?

B) Is there anything I need to say sorry for? Will You forgive me?

C) Is there anything You want me to pray for?

D) Jesus, do You have any promises or blessings for me?

SAY: There's another way we can love God with our mouths, and that is by using them to speak kind words to others instead of hurtful words. Can you think of a time when you said something that wasn't right? Read Psalm 34:13 together. Try saying the verse out loud while holding your tongues! Talk about ways in which your child could use his or her mouth to love God.

Prayer

Thank You, God, for loving me! Help me to show You love by listening to You and talking to You. Help me to always use my mouth for good things, not for bad. Amen.

We Love God through Worship

Worshiping God is one wonderful way we can show God that we love Him, because in worship we are telling God how amazing He is.

SAY: One way to worship God is to tell Him all the things that He's super good at. Let's think of some things that God is good at and tell Him! (For example, God is loving and kind and the smartest and the strongest and the most powerful...)

SAY: Another way to worship God is by singing songs to Him and making music. Let's sing our favorite worship song together (or make one up). If you have children's instruments accessible, use them to have a little orchestra.

SAY: Another way to worship God is by reading Bible verses that talk about how amazing God is. Read Psalm 100 together, with your child repeating the words after you.

SAY: Another way to worship God with our bodies is to dance! Let's dance for God. (If you like, you can turn on some music or sing a worship song while you dance together, or just let your child dance to the music in his or her head).

You will need a piece of paper and a pencil. **SAY:** One more way to worship God is to draw pictures of the things we love about Him or write those things down. Let's do that now.

Prayer

Thank You, God, for loving me! Help me to show You love by listening to You and talking to You. Help me to always use my mouth for good things, not for bad. Amen.